Doggy Heaven

Doggy Heaven

Lessons Peaches Teaches

Dan E. Ferguson

Charleston, SC
www.PalmettoPublishing.com

Doggy Heaven
Copyright © 2022 by Dan E. Ferguson

First Edition

979-8-88590-659-3

Dedicated

To the dog I didn't want
Who was sure our family members
Talked about her
Whenever we mentioned
How the juicy fruit dripped
At Pike's Market in Seattle.

Contents

Introduction

••●••

Talk about dog trauma. Meet King, our family's German shepherd, who was poisoned by a neighbor because he got into her flower bed. Or our sheltie, Lindsey, who ran off three times. After the last time, we never saw her again. Chico, our Chihuahua, birthed twenty-two puppies in four different litters, and one little puppy barely survived.

Peaches, a hybrid mix of Maltese and poodle, returned to us after surgery for kidney stones with her insides still hanging out. The veterinarian was out of town. She refused to talk to us, and her assistant said she had no training to help. While Peaches was hanging on by a thread to life, my wife, Glenda, and I had no choice but to take her to an animal hospital fifty miles from home.

Peaches has been chased by a Doberman pinscher and a Jack Russell terrier and barely escaped a charging pit bull. She acted tough. Her feisty side never backed down to a dog twenty times her weight—she once chased a Rottweiler down the street. When her fur got shaggy, she had no intention of allowing anyone to groom her. She refused to allow Glenda to pick the matting from her eyes. She snapped to remind us of her rights. We tried ganging up on her, yet her stubbornness usually won the battle. All we could do was laugh at her persistence. The drama we endured with these dogs, however, drew us closer to the tail-wagging canines and served to unite our family.

Peaches would love to meet a celebrity who loves all dogs. Country singer Carrie Underwood won many awards for her recorded songs, but she deserved more for her dog-loving ways. She had quite an eventful evening on April 3, 2022, in Las Vegas. Carrie received her eighth Grammy for her first gospel album, *My Savior*—the Grammy was presented for the best roots gospel album. Husband Mike Fisher watched as Carrie performed "Ghost Story" for the first time, ascending high above the crowd in a purple, strapless gown with a flowing train. All that in one evening prompted her to exclaim, "I am eternally grateful!"

Underwood posted her joy on social media. She gushed, "I WON A GRAMMY!!!!! I love this album (#MySavior) so much and I truly believe it is the most important album I have ever made! Thanks to all who supported! I am eternally grateful! Glory to God! And I got to sing #GhostStory for the first time on the @recordingacademy stage! What a night! #Grammys #Blessed #Grateful"

Carrie highlighted just how important this album was to her. While fighting to hold back the tears, she said, "This is one thing I've literally wanted to do my whole career…This just means the world to me."

Arriving at home after the Grammys, she discovered an unexpected loss. Her rat terrier, Ace, was dead. She went from tears of joy to tears of sorrow. From gratitude to grief.

The next day, she posted on social media:

> *Last night my sweet Ace left this world…he will forever live on in our hearts and be forever missed.*
>
> *He was there for me when I was on my own trying to figure out life when it was at its craziest! He was with me through 3 houses, 6 tours, and 2 kids…always ready to snuggle and play…through all the highs and lows. He was a true friend*

and a good boy till the very end. I love you, sweet Ace...see
you on the other side...

Underwood posted photos of Ace on Instagram, one showing Carrie kissing Ace's head. Ace was always included as one of the family. An example occurred when Carrie was planning her wedding for July 10, 2010. Ace was pegged as one of the ringbearers, her nephew as the other. She told *People* magazine, "He's like my kid. Ace is such a big part of my life." The flower girl's job? She was responsible for holding Ace's leash.

Carrie's love for dogs has reached out to many more beyond Ace. She volunteered at a shelter in January of 2014. Referring to a couple of dogs at the shelter, she said, "One is trying to kiss me while one is trying to rip my scarf off!"

Besides Ace, Carrie showed her love to their dachshund mix named Penny. Both Ace and Penny accompanied Underwood when she toured on the road, but they didn't leave the bus.

Ace attained celebrity status, appearing with Carrie in an ad for Almay in January 2015 and on the cover of *Redbook* in November 2016. Ace was injured, sustaining a herniated disk that completely paralyzed his back legs. He was eventually able to recover the use of his legs through physical therapy, including water therapy.

Shortly before Carrie's son Jacob was born on January 21, 2019, a German shepherd was added to the family. Isaiah, four years older than Jacob, decided to name him Zero. Mike joked, "I guess it fits because it's the chance of surviving if you try to break into our home."

Carrie honored National Puppy Day with photos of all their dogs on social media, one picturing Ace wearing a diaper. And all three dogs once posed wearing Christmas sweaters. Kudos to Carrie Underwood for her unconditional love for dogs.

When childhood heroes Lassie and Rin Tin Tin vanished, we never saw them on TV again. Benji and Beethoven no longer starred in the movies. We felt a void. But thankfully, our culture began to shift.

Many charming dogs appear in the TV commercials we see today. A golden retriever runs through knee-high weeds and jumps into a kiddie pool full of water. A member of the most popular breed for the last three decades, a yellow Labrador retriever named Stevie, trained for six months to play the role of Mom.

Augie is a purebred golden retriever who dares to be arrested for driving without a license. A dog of many talents, he holds a world record for holding five tennis balls in his mouth at one time. A collie named Lassie jumps to rescue a man stuck in an elevator. Hudson, another golden retriever, has appeared in commercials for E-Trade, Coca-Cola, Macy's, and Febreze. He also played presidential candidate Mitt Romney on *Saturday Night Live* in 2012.

A white miniature bull terrier named Bullseye with a red circle around his left eye mimics a former star named Spuds MacKenzie. A dog named Duck is able to jump into the back seat of an SUV when he gets old because he ate the right dog food. Another dog is rescued, cared for by a veterinarian, and survives because he ate the competitor's dog food. Advertising dogs like Lulu and Lobo have conquered speaking so fluently in the English language. A local bank in Wichita advertises that if you open an account there, the bank will donate to a worthy dog charity.

As the most popular dog in the United States, golden retrievers are seen the most often in TV commercials. Next comes the golden

Lab because these two breeds project a clean image on the screen. A current trend leans toward using the Heinz 57 mutt in commercials, breaking away from featuring the purebred. If an advertiser wants to appeal to the common people, the mongrel reaches more of them in selling the product line.

Dog movies, as well, have skyrocketed in popularity. We meet new dogs with those romps on the big screen. Now we have almost as many dog stars as human heroes. Dogs are able to avoid finger pointing and politicizing, while a few human actors and actresses are not.

Advertisers and agents have good reason to feature dogs in their commercials. Realtor.com says 89 percent of millennials own a pet, and 79 percent of those millennials pass up the perfect house if it fails to meet the pet's needs. The marketing experts tell us that a commercial including a pet steals the viewer's attention.

These same statistics also verify that Americans now adore dogs. Not that they didn't before, but their love is currently more out in the open. Those giddy dogs sneak up on us when we least expect it and wrap us around more than any little finger; they gradually overwhelm all ten fingers and every appendage. Most of all, they take over our hearts.

During the years I was growing up, we always lived with a dog in our home. But the dog seemed to live in the background because of our time packed with activities, while our pets seldom received the attention they deserved. Unless they broke the rules.

The hardest page to turn is the one when the dog ages and eventually has to be put down. On the human side, I have been privileged to work with thousands of people who were journeying through the difficult maze of grief. Academic teaching about how to comfort the mourning didn't feel like lots of fun, but it provided options I wouldn't have perceived on my own. Schooling about working with the bereaved seemed useless if it couldn't be applied to loving people who were suffering.

Why can't someone help in the healing process for all who grieve after the death of a beloved dog? Bereaved dog owners need an extra dose of comfort. Scripture highlights some encouraging words pointing to a place in heaven for those dogs we miss so much.

In the book *Love Is the Best Medicine: What Two Dogs Taught One Veterinarian about Hope, Humility, and Everyday Miracles*, the words of Dr. Nick Trout warm my heart. Trout says, "At veterinary school we become indoctrinated in the church of the scientific method, accepting the gospel according to rational thought and proven data."[1]

Trout then reverses that theme to share what worked for him. He says, "For all the fancy technology and medical advances, what endures and what will always matter most is the intensity of the relationship between human and animal…Fundamentally, our professional goal is to repair and sustain mutual love."[2] His words underscore my thoughts about how academics and compassion work hand in hand. But love always wins in the long run.

You may love your dog so much that you talk to it as you would a person. Some dog owners try to cover their tracks by quickly denying ever talking to a dog. Their conversation sounds like this.

"Do you talk to your dog?"

"No, I would never talk to my dog."

"Sure you don't."

Whether you deny or confess it, most of us talk to our dogs. Those who do talk to their pets find themselves in an elite class. One scientific study reveals that those who talk to animals are smarter than those who don't. One recent study by Gary D. Sherman and Jonathan Haidt of Harvard University found that people who love animals and talk to their pets are more intelligent than those who do not.[3] People who talk to their dogs are not childish or crazy.

Sherman and Haidt's study concentrated on people's ability to attribute human characteristics to animals or objects that are not human. The technical term, anthropomorphism, refers to childhood play: conversing with pets, dolls, stuffed animals, and other inanimate objects. A child is able to give these pets and objects names and talk to them.

The results of this study by Sherman and Haidt are confirmed by Nicholas Epley, professor of behavioral sciences at the University of Chicago. Epley affirms that this practice during childhood is not something to make fun of but in the long run shows up in people who are smarter than those without it.

I'm all for anything that will make me appear smarter. It's so comforting to know that we won't star in *Dumb and Dumber* when we talk to our pets. That habit does not make us childish, stupid, ill, or crazy. Even though it's been my habit for a long time, I can do so with much more confidence now. Allow me to put my new smart pill into practice.

Say Peaches has been sleeping in for a couple of hours after I woke up. "Are you ready to get up, little buddy?" I ask. She awakes, and my IQ jumps well beyond any previous level.

When I communicate with Peaches, she usually understands and has her own way of interacting with me sans words. "What is she barking about?" Glenda, my wife, asks with a puzzled look on her face.

Peaches has a built-in volume control among her barks and moans; they project different meanings. Her loudest bark is for people food, especially for ice cream or donuts. A medium bark indicates it's time for a walk, and the softest bark tells us someone is ringing the doorbell when we can't hear it downstairs. When she moans or whines during sleep time, she is dreaming. And with her separation anxiety, she sometimes moans when left alone.

When Peaches scratches at her water dish, she is relaying the message that she needs water. Her dish has always been empty when she makes that noise. The same goes for when she is on a trip with us and she is thirsty. At that time, she scratches at the tiny compartment underneath the dashboard where we keep a tiny cup just her size. We have prepared for her request with water in the car for her to drink. When she scratches at my leg, she is usually telling me she would appreciate a bite of my healthy oatmeal for breakfast.

Peaches isn't equipped to smile but exuberantly shares her joy by spinning in circles. Or when she is outdoors, her happiness is evident when she runs fast or hops through the grass. Indoors, she shows her joy during playtime by running in circles.

Much like a spouse, who over time learns to think like and anticipate the thoughts of a mate, I have learned to understand what Peaches tries to communicate with me. I simply wish some people communicated with me as well as Peaches does.

Peaches tries to talk to us but only goes as far as moving her mouth like any talking human. We know she has something important to say when we see her jaw moving up and down. It would be fun to create a video, dubbing her words in. She could upgrade her resume, morphing into a star like those dogs on TV.

Back in my younger days, I ran a lot, participating in marathons, 10K races, one-mile races, and all—all that mileage adding up to a cumulative distance of well over a trip around the world at the equator. On rare occasions, I ran with someone, but usually it was just me alone pounding the pavement or the rocky roads. One late, sunny afternoon, I was running on a rocky, deserted road two miles from home. This was in barely civilized farm country where humans seldom appeared. Except on that day, I ran by an old man, his rattletrap of a car, and his mangy old mutt.

I didn't think much about it, got to the turnaround, and started back toward home. The old man and his car were along the road, but where was the dog? I soon found out when he sneaked up behind me, jumped up, and took a bite out of my wrist. The dog was detained at the police department to make sure it didn't have rabies, and the law said I had to go to the local police department to file a report. All the while, I fretted over whether or not I would arrive at a meeting six miles away on time. After three days in his own prison, the test results on the dog turned out negative.

Soon after that, a running friend coached me to take a couple of actions when confronted by a threatening dog on the road. The first directive suggested that I position my body so that the dog encountered me face to face, so that I was staring the dog down. The second was to yell loudly, "Back off."

The test came a couple days later when I was running down another rocky road about five miles from home. I could see a house about three hundred yards down a driveway from the road. Suddenly, two black Labs came racing down the driveway toward me. I turned to face them and yelled, "Back off." They turned around and slowly loped back toward the house. In contrast, it would be wise not to challenge a dog whose very breed is known for violence.

On a more positive note, a dog offers a multitude of benefits to a home, office, hospital, nursing home, war zone, or police station. "These days, we're all stressed," a current TV commercial proclaims. Research has shown that dogs have a knack for reducing stress in the home or workplace. When we arrive at home after a long day at work, who do we find happy to see us? Other members of the family have had their own stress to deal with during the day, so it's usually not them. The dog, though, never fails to be happy to see us.

Current research has shown that dogs boost our health quotient. They have a part in lowering our blood pressure, minimizing heart disease, and successfully diminishing the effects of mental disorders such as anxiety, depression, and posttraumatic stress disorder. They boost our self-esteem and lift our morale. Dogs frequently make us laugh; stay tuned to find examples of their humor in these chapters. Research has validated that laughter also heals.

The American Heart Association has shown that dog owners spend more time on physical exercise while minimizing their loneliness and depression. In a recent study, the AHA proved that dog owners recover more often from a heart attack or stroke than those who don't live with a dog.[4] The study was led by the National Patient Register of Sweden. Canine keepers had a 33 percent higher chance of recovery after a heart attack if they lived with a dog.

The *Washington Post* highlights ten recent studies found in *Circulation*, a publication of the *American Heart Association*. Cardiologist Dhruv Kazi of Beth Israel Deaconess Medical Center in Boston warns of going so far as to believe it's only the dog that causes better heart health.

"Pet owners tend to be younger, wealthier, better educated, and more likely to be married, all of which improve cardiovascular outcomes,"[5] writes Kazi.

While cat owners also had better health than those without cats, another of these AHA studies found that dog owners were happier than cat owners.[6]

Peaches never failed to bark loudly enough to remind me it was time for our daily walk. Because of her age of fourteen human years, walking as far as we used to has gradually transformed into more of a challenge for her. But she still prodded me to exercise and to breathe fresh air each day. She never allowed me to slack. She kept me accountable. My gratitude overflowed toward Peaches for taking care of me in that way.

Consider the contrasts of a dog's life.

Dogs can be annoying, but they never talk back, never argue.

Dogs can be ornery, but we wouldn't want them to lack spirit.

Dogs can bite, but more often they are healers who make a positive impact on our health, including that of our most essential organ, the heart, as well as our mental health.

Dogs can add stress to our lives, especially when we try to train them, but more frequently they reduce our stress.

The life of a dog is short compared to that of a person, but dogs' kindness lengthens our lives. Many times, dogs have saved the lives of humans, and they have at times prevented people from needing mental health counselors.

Dogs can run away from home, but they also remain loyal to their owners, sometimes much more loyal than people.

Dogs can be contrary, but they can also be obedient.

Dogs can plunge into an abundance of mischief, all the more to make us laugh.

Dogs can be expensive, but all the love they give us makes their gifts worth the cost.

Dogs rescue people, though some humans are convinced it's the other way around.

Some of my friends say they don't want any dog. "Too much work. You have to find someone to watch the mongrel when you go out of town," they complain. "The cost sets you back too much. A dog takes way too much of your time." There is a grain of truth in their allegations.

But thank God an opposing group of friends knows the joy and love dogs offers all canine parents.

1

..●..

No More Dogs

"No more dogs," Glenda lamented, struggling with her grief.

Six months earlier, my wife had listened to the veterinarian tell us that the stomach cancer of our sheltie, Lady Luck, had spread. Her pain was too obvious. We had reached the painful moment when we felt we had no choice but to allow the vet to put her down. No longer could we bear to watch Lady's suffering and confusion. We reluctantly consented to allow the vet to end her life on planet earth.

If that wasn't bad enough, we had had to suffer through the same grief with Lacey, our Chihuahua, just three months before Lady's death. We were crushed by the look of fear in Lacey's eyes before she was euthanized. With no warning, we fell into a dogless plight. Our struggle didn't end immediately. Every time we arrived home, thinking we needed to let the dogs out, we felt a jab of pain. Good memories we cherished, but even they brought a twinge of grief and some tears.

After the deaths of both dogs, Glenda wasn't planning on going through the same pain of bereavement again. "No more dogs," she wearily whispered.

Not that Glenda hadn't said those very words over and over before when we mourned the loss of a dog. But in the midst of the time she mourned, those words didn't last long.

"No more dogs," I echoed. But my reason for those words was different from hers. "After all, isn't moving enough stress without the chaos of training a new puppy? Don't you remember all the work that takes?"

Not only were we grieving the loss of two dogs, but we were also mourning the loss of close friends as we prepared to move. Having already moved twenty-one times in my lifetime, I was acutely aware of the stress, sweat, and decision making awaiting us with the move.

I jumped overboard on the side of discipline; my feet were set in the sand. Don't cross that line, I thought. I frowned with my most serious look, emphasizing it with an unconscious, audible sigh, a sigh the family would recognize as my normal sign of frustration.

Besides working at the hospital in skilled nursing in Coffeyville, Kansas, Glenda was moonlighting at a nursing home fifteen miles away in Independence. She just "happened" to stop by a pet shop on her way to work in Independence.

Suddenly, her tune began to change. Glenda's new stance surprised me. "Don't you think we need a puppy?" she asked.

"I found the perfect dog for us. She is a white Maltipoo with peach-colored ears. She is soooo cute!" Glenda exclaimed, her voice reaching a new octave higher than normal with excitement.

I held my ground. That she had spotted a lapdog—half Maltese, half poodle—had not impressed me.

When Glenda found me less than enthusiastic about this puppy, she immediately summoned our daughter, Andrea, a senior in high school at the time. Of course, she didn't bother to let me know she was going for reinforcements. "Andrea, you've got to see this puppy in Independence! She is soooo cute!" Glenda shrieked.

Andrea was not a hard sell. Since she was all of four years old, she had repeatedly said, "I just want a puppy I can hold in my hand."

My previous animosity for poodles added to the big picture. I had voiced my strong feelings toward poodles many times. "I don't want any poodle. Too prissy for me!" I insisted.

Even half a poodle was going to be a problem for me. In my mind it was all settled. Yet it really wasn't. No deal.

The next scene features me all stretched out on a beanbag, watching TV. In walked Andrea, holding a tiny white furball. "Dad, do you want to hold her?" Andrea said, in her most soothing voice.

"No, put her in the utility room," I grumbled.

Glenda named her Peaches because of the way her ears had an orange tint in contrast to her cream-colored body. The dog experts call her ears the color of apricot, but we couldn't name her Apricot. Peaches would work. The name must be fairly common, since we have met three other dogs named Peaches since Glenda named our dog.

She had heavy, silky fur with a poodle's slightly rounded head and the black button nose and steely, dark brown eyes of a Maltese. She was born February 25, 2005, just eleven days after Suzy, my mother's dog, was born on Valentine's Day. Suzy ventured into life as a dachshund.

Peaches' tiny paws weren't heavy like those of some bigger dogs. Three months old by then, she tipped the scales at a hefty eight ounces when Andrea brought her home. The Maltese breed is one of the thirteen tiniest dogs.

Peaches was never one to bark a lot. She was so quiet that she got stepped on at times when we were focused on washing and drying laundry in the utility room. She would yelp then, but as she got older, she wouldn't make a peep. When she got bigger, she was so quiet she would artfully sneak out the door behind us when we were leaving the house. And she knew enough to tiptoe behind us so that we couldn't hear her. We learned to look for her and bring her back inside, happy that we never drove off and left her alone.

"She is so cute!" We still hear that from strangers on the sidewalk or in a parking lot. She is ninety-eight in dog years, and we still hear how cute she is.

This stubborn dad didn't pay a cent for her, something I've been reminded of quite often. Glenda and Andrea pooled their money to pay the pet shop. They footed the entire bill for her. Not fair, especially when Peaches gravitated toward following me around in her later years. I have tried to make up for it by buying her food, shots, medications, grooming, a bed, a leash, and other supplies.

Glenda's father, Charles, had great skill when choosing a greyhound to race and hunt alongside. His greyhounds won lots of races. Charles repeated his advice many times to Glenda about picking the right dog. He said, "Always choose a female."

In choosing Peaches, Glenda obeyed. As a young child, Rachel, our older daughter, counted the males and females, including dogs, in the family. With Peaches adopted as a member of the family, Dad became outnumbered four to one. Rachel said, "Dad is numbered out."

In her younger years, I wasn't a member of Peaches' fan club, and she wasn't immediately included in mine.

Robert Fulghum, of *All I Really Need to Know I Learned in Kindergarten* fame, writes a witty story that I have condensed while trying to remain true to his storytelling skills. It is from his *Maybe (Maybe Not)* collection.

A man and a woman fell in love. She was forty, and he was fifty. They were old enough to see that their friends' marriages often struggled, so they crafted a prenuptial agreement. He was not enthused about dependent relationships, especially not with dogs. She liked taking care of children and dogs. Consequently, the prenuptial agreement said children or dogs, but not both.

She made her choice and bore two children. When the children reached school age, she jumped in with both feet to raise money through an auction that would help finance the art and music programs at her children's school.

The mother knew a lot about dogs and pedigrees, so she started shopping for the perfect dog for the auction. After a month of shopping, she found the "wonder dog," probably a mix of a black Lab and Weimaraner. She informed her husband that they would have to keep the dog "temporarily" for a couple of days. Then she took care of the dog's shots and bought supplies, spending a total of $260.

Fulghum writes, "'DOG,' as the father named it, has a long, thick rubber club of a tail, legs and feet that remind him of hairy toilet plungers, and is already big enough at four months to bowl over the girls and their mother with its unrestrained enthusiasm."[1]

On a Thursday night, the auction got off to a great start with many items on the auction block. "DOG" came up for auction early, as she had already eaten the leather cover on the steering wheel and crunched holes in the padded dashboard of their car.

The mother sat onstage and held "DOG" while the bidding heated up for the mongrel.

"What am I bid for this wonderful animal?" asked the auctioneer. "Now $100—now 200—now 250."

Mother began to weep. "Jack, I can't sell this dog—I want this dog—I love her," she sniffled through her tears and trembling voice.

Everyone in the room watched as the drama unfolded. Fulghum writes, "The father feels ill, realizing the bowling ball of fate is headed down his alley."[2]

With no fear of winning the bid, several men went for the record. No one was surprised when Jack won the bid at $1,500.

His wife hurried off the stage and threw her arms around Jack.

After a few days, Jack was seen around the neighborhood being pulled by his mammoth, high-dollar dog late at night. The dog had grown enough to plow now and "may be the world's dumbest dog, having been through obedience school twice with no apparent effect."[3]

Jack couldn't believe it. We had an agreement in the prenuptial, he thought. Children or dogs, but not both. "The love boat always leaks."[4]

With gratitude to Robert Fulghum for this masterpiece, I can say that it reminds me of my own journey.

Looking back, I could have been more sensitive to the needs of Glenda and Andrea. More loving, less stubborn, not as locked in on the moving plans. Andrea and Glenda may have felt my disciplined approach was too harsh.

Saint Paul offers guidance to remind me to act better the next time. He writes, "Fathers, do not provoke your children to anger" (Eph. 6:4, New Revised Standard Version). Andrea must have gotten over it—I know because of the many kindnesses she showed later on and a thank-you note that said she hit the parent jackpot.

I wasn't quite ready to give my heart to any pipsqueak of a puppy. And there was some dog drama from my past to deal with first.

The balancing act to discipline is love. Children and pets gently chip away at stealing our hearts. Ask any grandparent; that person will tell you discipline doesn't rate as high as it used to. But love does.

Glenda gave Peaches her name because of these orange ears.

2

•• ● ••

King Survives

Dogs, as you know, have been called "man's best friend." But they can add some trauma to our lives. Not only did I dread dealing with moving at the same time we were training a dog, but some unpleasant memories also continued to haunt me.

During my ninth-grade year, we moved to the west side of Wichita. Our new ranch-style house had acres behind it where my grandparents planted a mammoth vegetable garden. They had wanted to raise tomatoes, corn, green beans, cucumbers, and lettuce for decades but lived in a large house with a yard the size of a postage stamp. That garden grew into a team effort of the entire family.

In front of the house was a sandy road called Sierra Drive and a barbed wire fence separating that road from Airport Road. I played basketball with a neighbor boy my age and his cousin a year older. The mother of the boy my age cultivated gorgeous roses of many colors in front of their house.

I thought we had a good relationship with that family. They trusted us to enter their house and feed their fish when they were out of town, adding a few dollars for our efforts when they got home.

My brothers and I were excited when my stepfather, Ken, brought home a German shepherd soon after we moved in. Ken named him King. We had lots of space to run King—sometimes on foot, sometimes by car—in our neighborhood near the airport. King got used to the roar of jets landing and taking off overhead, as did we. The flying aircraft didn't cause him to bark or us to shudder. We became oblivious to the sound of thundering jets approaching for a landing and planes departing in the "Air Capital of the World."

German shepherds are often employed as service dogs. Their name in German, *Schutzhund*, means protection dog. According to the American Kennel Club, the German shepherd is an intelligent dog with moderate energy. The AKC says that the German shepherd is "a loyal family pet and a good guard dog, the ideal choice for many families." The AKC also stresses the need for basic obedience training for this breed. Ken supplied some training, teaching King to sit, heel, and follow other commands.

King made a good watchdog because he projected a scary, deafening bark when a stranger approached. He took his job as guardian of the house seriously. On the other hand, he was gentle and loving to everyone in our family and would never be anything but friendly to children who came to visit us.

Framed by some sable coloring over his black body, King seldom entered the home but lived in an open-air garage separate from the house. Through a doorway with the door removed, he had access to the entire backyard, which was enclosed by a four-foot chain-link fence.

More than once, King made the mistake of escaping from the garage and our adjoining backyard. We could never find any evidence that he had dug a tunnel under the fence, so he must have gone over. Twice, the neighbor lady let us know that he had found his way to her beautiful flower bed. Her roses had been trampled down. We looked for a scapegoat, but there were no children in our neighborhood who could have done the damage. And the older kids knew better. We could eliminate the possibility that it was an act performed by a stranger in the neighborhood. We deduced only King could be the culprit.

One evening, our family discovered King outside the fence, lying on his side. We saw that he was foaming at the mouth with his eyes shut. He was gasping for air. We feared the worst. He might not survive.

This was worse than any illness. Who could have done this evil act? With no one we knew to blame, we focused on our first priority—to take care of King. Although we had no concrete evidence to prove it, we jumped to the conclusion that the neighbor lady with the bed of roses poisoned him. And we had seen the daggers in her eyes.

King was near death, hanging on by a tiny thread. Ken, my brothers David and Stan, and I stayed close beside him throughout the night, feeling as though those hours of darkness would never end. We bore King's torture with deep, intense sympathy. We prayed that he would somehow come back to acting like himself, but the chances looked slim. We were overwhelmed by fear that he would not make it through the night.

Stan was always King's sidekick, the one King went to first. But it was David who kept the faith that King would survive. Somehow, in ways we could never explain, a miracle took place on Sierra Drive in the early morning hours. We were so grateful that King slowly began to act like himself again.

Ken said, "If it hadn't been for David's faith through the night, King wouldn't have been able to pull through it."

After the long, grueling night, we celebrated that King had overcome!

Stanley Coren has rated which breeds are the smartest in his book *The Intelligence of Dogs: A Guide to the Thoughts, Emotions, and Inner Lives of Our Canine Companions.*[1] Coren didn't act alone, surveying almost two hundred dog-obedience judges to obtain his results, which are based on instincts, obedience, and the ability to adapt. German shepherds came out third of all breeds. We just wished King had been smart enough to steer clear of the flower beds.

Unfortunately, in a similar case, dogs belonging to the Cornwall family in Las Vegas didn't fare as well. Living in a neighborhood close to Sahara Avenue and Fort Apache Road, the family said someone tossed poisoned meat over the family's wall.

Their dogs, Laya, Luke, and Chervey, ate some of the meat, which had poisonous seeds strategically placed inside. The dogs soon started to have seizures, so the family hurried them to the vet.

Laya passed away that same evening, and the other two were in critical condition, one of them unable to walk. The Cornwalls, as reported by KSNV-TV, said, "We can't understand why someone would do something so cruel."[2]

The same senseless, cruel attacks have also occurred at dog shows. In an article by veterinarian Justine Lee in *Pet Health Network*, it was reported by the *Huffington Post* that several dogs (including a Shih Tzu, a West Highland white terrier, and an Afghan hound) became ill at the Crufts Dog Show in Birmingham, England.[3] According to the *Daily Beast*, some show veterinarians got concerned that some of the dogs might have been poisoned.[4]

One show dog named Jagger, a prizewinning Irish setter, keeled over and died soon after arriving home in Belgium. The results of an autopsy revealed that Jagger's stomach contained beef infused with poison.

These poisonings are no isolated cases. According to the WebMD Pet Health Center, in 2020 more 232,000 cases of dog poisonings were reported in this country.[5] Some are intentional; some accidental. Because of the brutality of some inhumane people, stopping the intentional poisonings looks almost impossible. Only a miracle will change the hearts of these cruel bullies. Since King was poisoned, however, I have become more defensive about ending the accidental poisonings.

Dr. Justine Lee has served as associate director of veterinary services at the animal poison control center in Minneapolis, Minnesota. Lee has also taught at the University of Minnesota College of Veterinary Medicine. She points out ten common groups of household items that could accidently cause poisoning in a pet.

Prescription medications for people. Poisoning does not require a large dose either. Prescription anti-inflammatory drugs and pain medications cause vomiting and serotonin syndrome, a dangerous threat that elevates temperature, heart rate, and blood pressure and causes seizures.

Insecticides—flea and tick products.

Over-the-counter medications—Tylenol, Ibuprofen, Advil, Aleve, fish oil, and joint supplements.

Pet medications—drugs from the vet, including painkillers and antiworm meds.

Household products—cleaning products and fire logs can cause stomach and respiratory problems and vomiting.

People food—nuts, guacamole, onions, garlic, grapes, raisins, coffee, other caffeine, alcohol, and artificial sweeteners.

Chocolate—dark chocolate is worse than milk chocolate. In smaller dogs, one half ounce of baking chocolate can be fatal. The above items can cause a rapid drop in blood pressure, seizures, and liver failure.

Plants—azaleas and rhododendrons contain toxins that can cause diarrhea, vomiting, and coma. Tulip and daffodil bulbs may cause stomach problems, difficulty breathing, and an increased heart rate. A few seeds of sago palms may cause vomiting, seizures, or liver failure.

Rodenticides—not only should we keep a dog from rat and mice poisons, but we must also watch to prevent the dog from eating a poisoned rodent.

Lawn and garden products—keep dogs away from fertilizer, weed killers, and chemicals.[6]

Other items to be on guard for include antifreeze and gasoline. This is just the short list, as Wikipedia itemizes a few more, including currents, fruit pits (apple, peach, ,plum, or persimmon),chives, leeks, as well as plants oleander, castor bean, and hemlock..[7] If your dog will eat anything, like some we have owned, you are advised to watch the dog closely.

Should your dog be acting unusual and you wonder whether it has gulped down something toxic, here are some down-in-the-dumps results that follow poisoning: foaming at the mouth, unrestrained drooling, no appetite, lethargy, vomiting, diarrhea, high pulse rate, pale gums, excessive thirst, frequent urination, lack of coordination, trouble breathing, tremors, muscle twitching, seizures, passing out, and coma.

Like the Hartwells who lost Laya, many people find it a challenge to understand how anyone can be so cruel as to poison a dog. The Bible offers a contrast between those who take care of their animals and those who are cruel to them. It reads, "The righteous care for the needs of their animals, but the kindest acts of the wicked are cruel" (Prov. 12:10, New International Version. All future references are from the NIV unless otherwise noted.)

Evil hearts will have to change before deliberate poisonings will end. Dogs deserve much better. But if this chapter has been able to save even one dog from a deadly poisoning, the goal has been achieved.

Because it is natural to question what makes people who are cruel to pets tick; let us now look at a few reasons for their hard-to-swallow brutality.

3

••●••

Fear the Dogcatcher

Fear. The trembling emotion that had swept over the entire Wichita community when I moved back in 1979. It was like a huge cloud hanging over the whole city, invading our peace of mind. Anxiety. Depression. Terror. It felt as if a tornado was headed for the city to blow up people and buildings. The pessimist had to believe God wanted no part in this picture. A serial killer kept taunting the police and people throughout the city with clever prose and poetry that appeared daily in the newspaper and on television. Police were searching day and night for a lead that would point to an end to the madness.

Every evening, the television news clip pictured a gurney carting a body bag that covered a member of the Otero family. The family member was being wheeled out of the house by John Rodda from Cochran Mortuary. The psychopathic executioner had killed four people in the Otero family, including eleven-year-old Josephine and nine-year-old Joseph Jr. The two children would have been driven to Allen Elementary School a few minutes later. Charlie (age fifteen), Danny (fourteen), and Carmen (thirteen) were all in school—fortunate to be spared from the violence, unfortunate to be confronted with the shock of witnessing the aftermath.

The killer's handwritten notes, printed regularly in *The Wichita Eagle*, played a game of cat and mouse—catch me if you can. By this time, the BTK Strangler had publicly claimed he had murdered three more women in their early to midtwenties.

He had created his own moniker—BTK, standing for "bind, torture, kill." The news publicized that the criminal was known to cut phone lines before entering the homes of targeted victims he had meticulously planned to kill.

Meanwhile, I was living alone in a parsonage with a pea-green shag carpet in the living room and no furniture. A friend loaned me a thick piece of foam rubber long enough to sleep on. Another friend offered me a card table and a couple of folding chairs to furnish the kitchen. My dad got some new furniture and brought a leftover up-holstered chair and lamp for the bare living room. Then I married Glenda for her elegant furniture, which Dad loaded into his pickup and horse trailer. Voila! I was fixed up with furniture. Granted, I found many other good reasons to marry her.

Before the wedding, I volunteered to serve as a police chaplain for the Wichita Police Department. One or two twenty-four-hour shifts a month, I was on call to drive a police department car to wherever the dispatcher sent me. The shifts ran from noon one day to noon the next day.

One twenty-four-hour shift was almost more than I could handle. At two in the afternoon, I officiated a funeral for a stillborn baby bur-ied inside a thirty-three-inch white casket. Heartbreak. At five thirty that evening I drove to three different locations to comfort a sister, mother, and father, explaining to them that their twenty-year-old sister and daughter had been found in a field after being murdered.

At midnight, dispatch sent me alone to counsel a paranoid schizo-phrenic single male. Some cover would have been appreciated. At one in the morning, I was sent to comfort the parents of a nineteen-year-old male who had plowed his car into a bridge after leaving a concert stoned. He did not survive. At six o'clock in the morning, I was asked to drive a woman who had been married sixty years to the hospital to identify her deceased husband. But I slept well the next night.

After journeying through some scary situations, I visited the fire-arms range and tried to qualify to carry a gun. But no such luck. During this time, I even fantasized about becoming a case-solving detective. Reality says I wouldn't have lasted long in that role.

I was reading *In Cold Blood* by Truman Capote and discovered I was acquainted with two of the people in the book: Reverend Leonard Cowan, who officiated at the funerals of the Clutter family in Garden City, and criminal attorney Russell Shultz, who defended killers Richard Hickock and Perry Smith. Later, I would meet relatives of the Clutter family in western Kansas. I also read *The Mullendore Murder Case*, by Jonathan Kwitny, during this time. Reading those books in the middle of the night, alone, didn't help my frame of mind any.

I soon got caught up in the local drama. Ever since BTK had started making the headlines, I had started going straight to the phone when arriving home. One Sunday evening after dark, I got home from church and immediately hurried to the phone. Silence. No dial tone. I ran across the street to consult a neighbor who had a collection of guns and knew how to use them.

"There's no dial tone on my phone, and it's giving me the creeps!" I blurted out.

"By God, if he's in there, I'll take care of him," he answered.

We then searched the house. After we found no one, I walked my neighbor back to his house.

"If you ever get scared like that again, let me know, and I'll come back," he responded.

As a child, Dennis Rader lived out his psychopathic personality by torturing and hanging small animals. The technical term is *zoosadism*. In May of 1991, he was hired by the City of Park City as a compliance officer and dogcatcher. Misty King, one of his neighbors, protested that he killed her dog for no reason.[1]

You may ask, how could a town hire someone like that? The best answer is to say he fooled a lot of people. After his arrest, even his family was shocked. They saw him as the church administrative leader and Scout cubmaster, never suspecting his double life. Before his family knew his identity, his wife was reading the paper and noticed the handwriting of one of BTK's published notes. "You write a lot like BTK," she said, having no clue she was talking to the same person who was highlighted in the headlines.

Ever since the FBI began behavioral profiling during the seventies, childhood cruelty to animals has served as a sign forecasting later juvenile delinquency, violence toward people, and brutal criminal acts. Most serial killers have a history of torture and maiming of animals in their profiles. For example, Jeffrey Dahmer not only tortured and killed small animals during his childhood, but he also accumulated roadkill, dissected it, and got turned on by the leftover fragments.

The Boston Strangler, Albert DeSalvo, who murdered thirteen women, shot dogs and cats with his bow and arrow. Columbine slayers Dylan Klebold and Eric Harris bragged about mangling animals for kicks. Across the pond in England, all of the following tortured and killed animals in childhood: Moors murderers Ian Brady and Myra Hindley, who killed five children between ages ten and seventeen; Robert Thompson, who killed two-year-old James Bulger; and Mary Bell, the Tyneside Strangler, who the day before her eleventh birthday strangled a four-year-old and later a three-year-old.

While not every person who abuses a dog is a psychopath or serial killer, Mark Griffiths in *Psychology Today* finds more reasons human beings torture animals.[2] Animals are sometimes tortured to intimidate women and children to keep them quiet about domestic abuse in the family. Animal torture could occur as a result of one of eight sexual paraphilic disorders the *DSM-5* (*Diagnostic and Statistical Manual of Mental Disorders*, fifth edition) lists. Crushing an animal for sexual pleasure, called crush fetishism, is one example. These eight disorders require a monumental transformation for any hint of change to take place in that person's actions.

Animals have been tortured in the production of movies. As many as one hundred horses were killed in the filming of the blockbuster movie *Ben Hur* in 1959. The second-unit director ordered the horses to be killed if they as much as limped, with no opportunity given to consult a vet. Twenty-seven animals died during the production of the 2013 blockbuster *The Hobbit: An Unexpected Journey*.

Some people have gotten their pleasure by mutilating animals to shock other people. Animals have been maimed and killed when someone seeks revenge on another person or family. That was the reason King was poisoned. I wish the lady whose flowers King trampled had talked to us first before sending her message with poison. It might have been possible to construct more restraints to keep King in our yard.

The huge cloud of terror over Wichita finally lifted when the BTK Killer was arrested near his home in Park City on February 25, 2005. It had been over thirty years since he first murdered four members of the Otero family in 1974. After thirty-one years, the entire city of Wichita was no longer being gripped by the strong arm of fear.

At first, Rader pleaded not guilty but later changed his plea to guilty. In court, he described the murders in detail as calmly as if he were talking about tomorrow's weather. He remembered every detail with no hint of remorse.

More of Rader's targets thanked their lucky stars he wasn't able to complete his missions to kill them. BTK waited for Anna Williams for hours in her home but said he was "livid" when she didn't come home at the expected time. Rader gave up on that plan. A lady named Mary who lived near Broadway Street rose to the top of his list of targets but was thankful to escape his intentions. Rader explained that as he got older, he wasn't sure he was able to fight the younger victims off physically.

The families of his victims still grieve, wonder why, and battle with forgiveness. His daughter, Kerri Rawson, wrote a book titled *A Serial Killer's Daughter: My Story of Faith, Love, and Overcoming*. She describes her battle to forgive her father in the book.

Dennis Rader received ten consecutive life sentences without the possibility of parole for 175 years. He has taken up permanent residency at the El Dorado Correctional Facility. Thanks to the Wichita Police Department and many other law enforcement agencies, Wichita is a safer place to live.

Ironically, BTK exhibited in a more psychopathic way some of the similar traits as the dogcatcher in the 2001 movie *Lady and the*

Tramp II: Scamp's Adventure. That flick characterizes the dogcatcher as a villain who is short tempered, rude, and bossy. I knew people who heard Dennis Rader ask the question "Do you know who I am?" with a smug look on his face.

The dogcatcher in the movie looks like Don Knotts, chases Scamp and Angel, and captures Reggie and Scamp, locking them away in the dog pound. His enemies include a list of dogs: Scamp, Buster, Angel, Tramp, Jock, Lady, Reggie, Trusty, and the Junkyard Dogs. That dogcatcher yells, "You little mutt! I won't forget you! I'll lock you in the pound, I swear it!" The dogcatcher was outsmarted by the dogs.

The movie ends happily, as Lady and the Tramp are in love and caring for four puppies: three daughters who look like Lady and one son who resembles Tramp.

All dogcatchers are not as evil as Rader. Today, they have graduated to a more honorable title: animal control officer. They work long, exhausting hours, display courage in facing grave dangers, and show kindness to animals.

Shirley Zindler has set a commendable example as an animal control officer for over twenty-five years. She has served her job in many challenging ways: cleared guard dogs so police could make an arrest; rescued animals from fires, floods, and traffic crashes; assisted pets when they were forced to leave their dead owners behind; gotten wounded in a raid on a cockfighting operation; waded rivers in the dark on an animal rescue; and descended down a pipe for fifty feet to rescue a dog who had been wedged there for weeks.

Zindler has shown her love for animals by rehabbing dogs who had physical or socialization problems. She adds two more chores to her job. Zindler says, "I've helped abandoned dogs deliver their litters and stayed up all night feeding orphans."[3]

She loves her job. "There is such a need. I survive by focusing on the positives. Saving a life, improving life for a person or animal, finding a great home for a pet, rescuing those in need. Those are the things that keep me going,"[4] says Zindler.

Most animal control officers work a thankless job for which we could show a little more appreciation.

4

•• ● ••

Who's Training Who?

Glenda and I sat on each side of our three-year-old grandson, Bentley, at the circus. He loved it and didn't want to leave when the final curtain bow had been taken and the lights had blinked on again. "I want more circus," he said.

We saw tigers who, at the crack of the ringmaster's whip, stood up on only their back legs and walked. Five tigers rolled over on the ground at the ringmaster's command. Two of them were white tigers, and Bentley took his time shopping the stuffed animals for sale after the circus, deciding he needed a baby white tiger. This grandpa was impressed with his choice and couldn't say no.

We watched elephants, massive as they were, stand on all four hooves on a tiny circular metal stand. We saw miniature ponies who were trained to trot around an enclosed circle. They also lined up in a straight-line formation on command. They were rewarded with treats as soon as the command was carried out.

One tiny dog in a full-body costume was trained to lie down and play dead when the clown commanded. Other small dogs and cats would jump onto the backs of miniature ponies for a ride. Lots of dogs were trained to run up a slippery slide and jump over a crossbar.

For many years, dating back at least three centuries, poodles have been the main acts at a vast number of circuses and vaudeville shows.

Although it's a long shot, yet still possible, the poodles we saw performing may have been distant relatives to Peaches.

While watching these amazing feats, I had to wonder what kind of effort it took to train these animals. The circus we saw showed that the humans were definitely in control of the animals. The human trainers ruled over the animals and demonstrated dominion over them.

We are told in the creation account of the Bible that human persons are to "rule over fish, birds, livestock, all wild animals and those that crawl on the ground" (Gen. 1:26, 1:28). Different versions translate the Hebrew in other ways. The Message says people are to "be responsible for" these creatures. The New Revised Standard Version says we are to "have dominion over" the animals. Synonyms for *dominion* include *supremacy, sovereignty, control, authority, mastery,* and *command.* The Genesis text says that God said, "Let us make mankind in our image, in our likeness, so that they may rule over" the animals (1:26).

The trainers at the circus were certainly taking authority in ruling over the animals. That could be the key needed in training our dog. It all sounds so easy until you try to train a tiny puppy. Training a pet sounds easy until you try to teach a young dog new tricks. We kept Peaches in the utility room with its tile floor because it was so much easier to clean up than the carpet. But we still found her waste on the carpet.

When we delved into the painstaking job of house training, it required lots of hand towels, stain remover, paper towels, elbow grease, and patience. The hard-core trick of sticking her nose in the mess never worked for us. While cleaning up her stinking waste, we wondered if Peaches would ever get the hang of it; still, we persisted in training her.

It began to work gradually at first. We would think she had it mastered, and then we found another accident. After a few days, we found one more. We were overjoyed when she finally conquered it. And since she was six months old, she has not had more accidents, except for when she was extremely ill or dealing with the aging process. In following our directions, she refuted our fears and surpassed our expectations. She got to the place where she would bark and go to the garage door to let us know she needed to go outside.

Glenda worked with Peaches, teaching her to follow commands. Armed with a treat—sometimes a piece of her donut—Glenda was persistent in teaching Peaches to sit, walk on her two back legs, roll over, lie still on her side, and when in the mood, shake. It took more prodding to get her to shake. She didn't want anybody touching her precious paws—a common trait among the Maltese breed. When company showed up at our house, Glenda enjoyed showing off the tricks Peaches had learned.

We also were introduced to a new trick by our sister-in-law Cheryl, who had taught it to Kramer, their miniature schnauzer. My brother David, who holds three degrees from Oklahoma University, and his wife Cheryl are die-hard Sooner fans. Cheryl's sister Carla is a devoted fan of the Sooners' rival, the Oklahoma State Cowboys. Cheryl asks Kramer, "Would you rather be dead or a Cowboy?"

Kramer lies on his side and plays dead. Peaches was able to master the same trick with a different rival—our trick directed toward the Jayhawk-Wildcat competition.

I taught Peaches to wait for traffic when we were taking our daily walk. Although it is recommended to have just one master giving commands, I was the one who walked Peaches each day. Feeling the need to protect her from traffic on our busy streets, I would say "Stay" when approaching an intersection that we needed to cross and simultaneously extend my hand to indicate a stop sign. She always obeyed.

In our high-traffic neighborhood, we never had to worry about Peaches running into the street while moving vehicles were threatening her well-being. In the long run, it was impressive how quickly she learned. Peaches showed her intelligence at a young age. Train a dog at a young age, and when she gets older, chances are good she will remember what she learned.

A woman in our neighborhood had lots of cats and dogs inside her house as well as outside her house. She had endured some major criticism from her neighbors (not us), and in defense, she let me know that her pets didn't talk back to her. In her mind, that made the pets more important than people. That theory raised some red flags for me. Sure, pets become an important part of the family, but placing them a rung above humans sets up the wrong pecking order. She might give her animals the right to vote in the primaries and general elections, but the scriptures don't go along with that idea.

Not only does the creation account give human persons sovereignty, but none other than King David also proclaimed humans in command. David writes, "You [God] have made them [human beings] rulers over the works of your hands; you put everything under their feet: all flocks and herds, and the animals of the wild, the birds in the sky, and the fish in the seas. Lord, our Lord, how majestic is your name in all the earth!" (Ps. 8:6–9). Both the creation account and the psalmist emphasize that humans are to have control over the animals.

As we prepared to move, there were so many tasks to keep us busy; we didn't have lots of time to train our little puppy. Sorting our many belongings took up time. Hours flew by during arrangements with the movers. Days went by while we packed up our possessions.

Which of our possessions would go to the thrift store? Which ones would be placed at the curb for the trash man? Which ones would go into the corner for packing? Peaches wasn't learning much while we went about the busyness of preparing to move.

The key to training a pet is simply to take authority. An umpire or referee earns respect by showing confidence, by exerting the upper hand in every call made. A gifted speaker engages the listening ear through putting teeth, heart, and soul into each word. And trainers of circus animals demonstrate their control with each unmistakable, authoritative command. Likewise, a dog owner knows the pleasure of the pet's obedience only when the animal understands who is taking charge.

During training, it is paramount to refrain from violence toward the dog. A failure to follow commands never justifies physical abuse toward an animal. Even loud scolding causes fear, which will keep the dog uptight during future commands. And being too aggressive toward the dog can ricochet back to the handler with more brute force from the dog.

In reality, though, Peaches was allowed to take authority too often. She was doing a great job of training me. She went to the shelf where the treats are stored and looked up at them. She gave me a pleading look with her puppy dog eyes. She might as well have said it. "Don't you know what I'm after?" And I gave in. What was that about taking dominion over the animals?

I plopped down on the recliner, and Peaches felt comfortable lying between my knees when she offered a message. She scratched at the blanket over my legs. She might as well have said it. "Pull the footrest up, too." And I caved.

When she was cold and needed a blanket to cover up, again she scratched with her front paws. "Sure, yes ma'am."

When she had to potty at two in the morning, she barked loudly enough to wake me up. Usually, that required more than one bark for me to move. Because it was better than cleaning up if she went in the house, I dragged myself out of bed, felt around for the flashlight in the dark, climbed the stairs, tied my shoes, and unlocked the door for her to go outside. By the time we got there, I was wide awake for another day.

When she thought it time for a walk, she barked in an unusually booming woof and headed for the door where we exited. But some days, I was busy and she had to wait awhile.

The American Kennel Club has my dilemma captured so well. They have the Maltese half of Peaches pictured in their perfect description. They say, "Maltese are highly intelligent and know very well how to use their charm to get their way. If given the chance, they become easily spoiled. This isn't a problem to dog-savvy owners, but many pet owners will give in, often resulting in a pet with poor manners." I confess. She got spoiled, but not to the point of having bad manners.

Maltese were bred because Roman emperors strove for a dog that appeared a pristine white, a color they considered divine. The

Maltese breed originated on the Greek island of Malta, pictured as early as 500 BC on an ancient amphora (a tall jar with two handles and a narrow neck).

During the first century AD, Strabo wrote that aristocratic women loved the dogs. Maltese dogs were bred with tiny poodles and spaniels during the seventeenth and eighteenth centuries to produce hybrids.

The Maltese dog never feels cramped by small spaces. This dog stays active inside the house, a tiny yard, or a minuscule fenced-in area. Maltese dogs adapt well to living in apartments, duplexes, flats, or townhouses, so they are often cherished pets of city residents.

Lauren Cahn in *Reader's Digest* says the Maltese breed is "big on personality."[1] Maltese dogs' personality profiles overflow in their friendliness. No wonder Peaches had me wrapped around her little paw.

Cahn also points out three traits of all Maltipoos that come directly from the two breeds of poodles and Maltese. She says they are "hypoallergenic (no shedding), highly intelligent, and high energy."[2] After scanning many lists of characteristics of the breeds of Maltese and poodles, I found ten attributes that are exactly the same, word for word, for both breeds. Affectionate, agile, cheerful, companionable, fearless, fun-loving, graceful, independent, and playful. Neither breed is good with small children.

A couple more similarities are just a matter of semantics. "Pleasant and easygoing" in the Maltese seems similar to "good-natured" in the poodle. "A gentle personality" in the poodle is equivalent to "patient and never short tempered" in the Maltese. Now that you have heard the flattery that dog handlers give Maltipoos, it is easier to understand how this innocent bystander could spoil one.

Who's training who? OK, I'll own up to the truth. She has me well trained. Is it worth it? Let's save some chapters to answer that question.

Our former tour guide to Italy, Linda Broce, sent the following training rules on Facebook. The author remains anonymous but certainly understood how training works.

Rules of the House

(Regarding the Dog)

The dog is only allowed in certain rooms;

OK, the dog is allowed in all rooms but has to stay off the furniture.

The dog can get on the old furniture only.

Fine, the dog is allowed on all the furniture but is not allowed to sleep on the bed.

OK, the dog is allowed on the bed, but only by invitation.

The dog can sleep on the bed whenever he wants, but only at the foot.

The dog can sleep anywhere on the bed, but not on the pillow.

The dog can sleep on the pillow.[3]

5

Andrea's Crowd

Andrea helped Peaches escape her little cage at the pet store in Independence. Just after graduating from high school, Andrea moved in with girls she had bonded with since we moved to Coffeyville. This group of girls had been friends since the eighth grade, and they rented a house together. They lived near downtown, a little over a mile from our house. Peaches was three months old, and Andrea kept her at their house overnight. What could I say? After all, Andrea had helped pay for Peaches.

We missed Andrea at home, but she had reached an age when it was time for her to plan her own journey. From the parental perspective, it was a blessing for Andrea to be responsible for feeding Peaches and to have to clean up after the dog took care of business.

Peaches now had the opportunity to display her extroverted personality while living with Andrea and her friends. She bonded in a close relationship with each one of them, always enjoying making new friends, as every Maltese does. Peaches offered strangers her undivided attention while wagging her tail, and she loved the opportunity to treat these girls the same way.

The girls at Andrea's house all thought Peaches was so cute, but it was Maria who had a long-range plan figured out. She knew that Peaches was receiving lots of attention from everyone when the girls went out to a baseball game, to Wichita, to the River Run, or just to hang out around Coffeyville. She insisted on carrying Peaches around all the time. Accordingly, it was Maria who was the person at the center of attention when she was holding Peaches.

Peaches loved Andrea's friends, and they all fashioned a bed for Peaches inside a laundry basket. It also provided a wall to keep Peaches from wandering out, from sneaking out when the door was open and getting lost. Peaches was living with a creative group of girls—their own close-knit family. Peaches was at a curious stage, having to smell and investigate every nook and cranny, and as a result she jumped in as part of the action in their house. Peaches bonded with each of the girls, especially with Andrea, who took her along whenever she wasn't at work.

This lighthearted band of friends enjoyed their merrymaking together, as they had the previous five years. Peaches fit in with their fun-loving ways, smitten with her new role as mascot for the girls' in-crowd. This inner circle of girls earned a reputation for their spirit and laughs during their school years. They enjoyed spreading the laughs and joy.

Another dog who wished to share her happiness, turning heads, was a goldendoodle, as reported by Emily Younger of KSNW, Channel 3, in Wichita.[1] Paisley, age three, impressed boaters and Jet Ski riders alike with her skill of tubing at Table Rock Lake.

"All our dogs make us laugh, but she is hysterical," said Paisley's owner, Cheryl Wimberley.

Paisley displayed a bundle of energy and an independent mind of her own.

"She is so free spirited. When we go walk and let her off her leash, you can just see that she loves life," said Wimberley.

Paisley showed off her free spirit to Wimberley's sixteen-year-old daughter, Kylie, on a family vacation to Table Rock Lake near Shell Knob, Missouri.

Wimberley said, "We had the big tube that you tube on, and Ms. Paisley decided that was her tube and it was not going anywhere without her, so Paisley decided she was going to ride on it.

"She did fine on there. In fact, one day she tried to push Kylie off with her head. She was nuzzling Kylie that she could do it herself."

Wimberley stated that Paisley impressed many people with her tubing; Paisley was the prime chatter about the lake.

"Everybody around us that was in a boat or a Jet Ski literally stopped to watch her. Even the people who own Fish 'N Fun resort were on the dock, and they were getting pictures because they hadn't seen anything like that," she said.

Wimberley said she hopes Paisley's story will mushroom to bring happiness to others.

"Enjoy life, and make it what it is, and have fun and relax. That would be my message—just smile and laugh about certain things because it's all kind of funny," Wimberley said.

Peaches wouldn't mind getting to know Paisley, and the girls in Andrea's circle would enjoy Paisley's outlook and Cheryl Wimberley's perspective.

Peaches chewed on everything in sight during the time she spent with Andrea and the girls. She chewed up quite a few of Andrea's shoes, destroying her favorite pair. She demolished their purses. She gnawed away at wooden legs on the dresser; no stain would ever cover all the teeth marks in the grain of those dresser legs. She destroyed a ton of household items with her teeth. Peaches was cutting her teeth while she was growing and learning from these girls.

During her time with these girls, Peaches learned how annoying fleas can be as she got ambushed by the pesky insects. Glenda, whose work ethic stemmed from her farm-girl upbringing, went into attack mode. She devoted hours to picking fleas from Peaches' fur. She hit Peaches with her killer version of a chemical blitz. Glenda wasted no time disposing of the fleas and helping Peaches feel comfortable again.

This was just one example of Glenda's ability to clean all things. Many times, Glenda worked a double shift, six in the morning to midnight, as a nurse in a nursing home. Sometimes she worked double shifts on consecutive days. Often, at the end of the day, paperwork wasn't yet done, and she stayed into yet another shift until it was. Yet she always kept the house clean enough for Mr. Clean to show up and inspect it with white gloves.

All her friends teased her because they couldn't figure out how she could maintain such an immaculate, spotless house while working so many hours. Neither could I. But I appreciated her commitment to cleanliness. Her ability to conquer the fleas pestering Peaches was but a small part of the big picture.

Peaches' bond with Andrea grew deeper over the years. Whenever we told Peaches we were going to see Andrea, Peaches wagged her tail and went into her spin cycle. She overflowed with joy. Glenda and I have been amazed at how well Peaches remembered these places. When we drove Peaches to Omaha, as we came near to Andrea's house, Peaches started barking and turning circles a block away. We haven't said a word about how close we are.

Peaches responded the same way when we were beginning our visit at Andrea's workplace. We've been there many times, yet Peaches has remembered both her house and her office since the very first time we went to them. Peaches did the same bark and spin cycle when we drove to the house of our older daughter, Rachel. Peaches has never forgotten a place or person.

This puppy was family oriented, expressing her love to every member of the family. And she was the same way to Andrea's family of friends. Maltese dogs were bred to be companion dogs. They loved people and chose to stay close beside them.

While living near downtown, Andrea took Peaches with her to a baseball game. There she got into a conversation with Hannah, a friend of one of Andrea's friends. This young lady recognized Peaches, having seen Peaches in the pet shop in Independence. Soon after Hannah left that pet store, she pondered all the questions about whether she could buy Peaches. Could she afford her? Could she take care of her? What would her parents think?

But Hannah really wanted that little puppy who was so cute. After wrestling with all the above questions and more, she went back to the pet store set on buying Peaches. Much to her chagrin, Peaches was no longer for sale. Andrea had already bought her.

It turned out to be a blessing Andrea's father didn't know about it when she was in Independence buying a puppy. He would have tried to stop her. It all turned out much better than Dad's plan.

Andrea transitioned from our family to a new family made up of her friends, her peers. She took Peaches along with her to be a part of her new family. In a similar way, a military dog was forced by the perils of war to mourn his owner's death and later adjust to his new family. Hawkeye, a Labrador, was devastated when his owner was killed in a helicopter crash in Afghanistan.

Navy SEAL Jon Tumilson had served in the military for sixteen years after signing up in 1995. Hawkeye lying at the foot of his master's casket during the funeral was a picture we couldn't forget. Hawkeye touched many hearts.

Petty Officer Jon Tumilson's funeral was held August 26, 2011, at the Rudd-Rockford-Marble Rock Community School in his hometown of Rockford, Iowa. Hawkeye lay near the coffin, moaning throughout the service.

The tiny bit of good news in this story found Tumilson's longtime friend—Scott Nichols, along with his family—stepping up and adopting Hawkeye into their family. They transitioned into the new owners of Hawkeye, confirmed by Carol Darby, a public affairs officer at Fort Bragg.[2] Even though Hawkeye still continued to mourn the loss of the owner he had loved so much, it surely comforted him to know a loving family was willing to accept him.

Many folks have reached out in a similar way, adopting a rescue dog from an animal shelter and accepting it as part of their family. These same people have usually felt the unconditional love a rescue dog has to give. That family could say they needed the dog; the dog learned it needed the love of a family.

6

•• • ••

Lindsey Runs Away

A month before popping the question to Glenda, I chose Lindsey out of a litter my pastor had bred. Three Shetland sheepdog puppies frolicked on his living room floor when I fell for Lindsey. She was the biggest of the three shelties, the most spirited, and the dog who instantly won me over with her personality. The average weight for a Sheltie is sixteen pounds. Full-grown, Lindsey weighed thirty-three. Pastor Edgar Lindstrom supplied certification from a kennel that she passed as a thoroughbred.

Shetland sheepdogs have become renowned for their intelligence. Scottish shelties were bred from rough collies and Cavalier King Charles spaniels to keep stray sheep from wandering from the flock. The American Kennel Club reports that the sheltie adores "learning new tricks. Shelties are easy to train and are world-class competitors in obedience, agility, and herding trials." The AKC instructs, "The sheltie will reach his best potential as a companion when given training in basic manners at the very minimum."

PetWave identifies the Shetland sheepdog as "an all-around family dog." Shelties connect well with children and other pets. They have thick double coats and need weekly grooming. Lindsey shed piles of thick fur in all our consecutive homes. Our shelties were always upset during a rainstorm, barking and pacing as thunder boomed.

The first time Lindsey went missing, it was after dark, about nine one night in Coffeyville. I immediately fired up the Pontiac Sunfire and combed the streets for an hour. No luck. I finally gave up and went to bed, saying a prayer that we could find her the next day. The sun was barely over the horizon the next morning as I began driving the streets again in our neighborhood.

I kept looking toward wooded areas and creeks, but there were too many to walk them all. After thirty minutes, about to give up and head for work, I was desperate and again asked for divine help in my search.

Suddenly, in my peripheral vision, I spotted a sable-and-white blur creeping along to my left. How exciting when the lost has been found! She barely moved. Her pace would not keep up with that of any sluggish turtle. Wandering the streets throughout the night will wear even a fit dog down. I loaded her in the car, scolded her, and drove home. Strike one. Unfortunately, this would not be the last time our hearts would be broken by her disappearance.

We endured another close call. While we visited my mother over the Fourth of July weekend, two hundred miles from our house, Lindsey stayed home with the arrangement that our next-door neighbor was willing to watch her and take care of her. We left our side door to the garage open so that she could go into our fenced-in backyard. The neighbor would be able to see the garage and yard from his house.

A tornado came through Douglass and devastated houses two blocks from our house while we were three and a half hours away. The tornado did no damage to our house, but it opened the fence gate, and Lindsey got loose. Fortunately, the neighbor was able to find her and put her back in the garage. Strike two.

Peaches, however, was not a dog who ran off from us. At times, we became enthralled with some other errand or job when we let her out to take care of business. Did she run off? No, she would wait at the front door or garage door. I'm embarrassed to admit there were times she would wait for thirty minutes or an hour for us to let her in. So sorry, we were preoccupied, unloading groceries or involved with babysitting our grandson. Peaches always forgave, as if nothing had offended her. She was never one to hold a grudge. Lindsey stirred up a challenge to find her. Peaches never did.

Glenda's brother, Charlie, was both deaf and mute, but he didn't have a problem communicating strong emotions. He visited with his family and friends via sign language. He teased me by making fun of how I looked while praying in church. A perfect imitation. All in fun. I wasn't offended. While attending the Kansas School for the Deaf in Olathe, he mastered the art of upholstering. He not only gained monetary employment with that skill but also learned to roll and pleat Naugahyde for custom cars. His work appeared in national magazines, including *Rod & Custom* and *Hot Rod*.

When we needed a couch reupholstered, Glenda invited her brother to drive 150 miles, stay overnight with us, and put his skills into practice. He was hard at work on a Wednesday in our garage. Unbeknownst to him, our eleven-year-old sheltie got loose. After all, even if she had made lots of noise, he could not have heard her.

We searched the neighborhood on foot and by car. We listened for any sound of her bark and peeled our eyes in hopes of sighting her. We called at the tops of our lungs. In spite of her record of absenteeism, she had come home a lot more times than she hadn't. But this time she didn't come home. Her absence stretched into hours and days.

Despairing, we groped for last-ditch methods to bring her home. We posted signs at the local post office in the small town of Douglass. We went door to door in the neighborhood, asking whether anyone had seen her recently. We drove over a hundred miles on back roads, streets, and highways. Over and over, we prayed to God. In spite of all that, we never found one decent lead.

Finally, on Saturday evening, three days after she went missing, we received a phone call. A total stranger described a sable-and-white sheltie she had seen on a major highway seven miles north of us. Her detailed description left no doubt she had seen Lindsey. I drove up and down that highway. I drove all the back roads, as dust flew. I sang, "Country roads, take her home." Still no sign of her.

It is so painful to know your dog is somewhere in the wild with no idea where she is. So many questions throbbed at our hearts. Had a wild animal attacked her? Had she found food or water? What if someone picked her up and was mean to her? Would someone find her and provide a loving home for her? We had to stop worrying and pray that Lindsey would somehow be back at home with us.

But we never saw her again. Strike three was the most painful. Still today, thirty-one years after she disappeared, we drive down the same highway. We look toward the place she was last seen, remember her, and wonder where she ended up. We still try to let her go, wishing we had at least had a chance to tell her goodbye. But should all dogs go to heaven, we look forward to seeing our sable-and-white sheltie again.

A more recent doggy death is hard to swallow. Lots of people in the city of Wichita and the state of Kansas are mourning the death of one of its most loved creatures. Millie the Weather Dog was seen on TV in front of the news desk, signing off at the end of each evening newscast on Channel 12. Millie starred on KWCH TV as the dog of Chief Meteorologist Ross Janssen. Millie, who passed away at age fourteen, was the perfect representative of the Pembroke Welsh corgi breed.[1]

The same breed that Queen Elizabeth II was so enthralled with since she was a small child, Pembroke Welsh corgis are known for their easygoing nature and loyalty. This breed was also a major influence in the lives of the queen's parents, King George VI and Queen Elizabeth I. They made sure the daughter who would become Queen Elizabeth II received her first corgi on her eighteenth birthday in 1944. Since Queen Elizabeth II came to power in 1952, she has owned more than thirty dogs of the corgi breed.[2]

Corgis are blessed with a ton of personality. The American Kennel Club tabs them as "smart and alert, affectionate but not pushy, bold but kindly."

They have the ability to adjust to any environment, have a need for daily exercise, and respond well to training. The AKC says, "The time you spend in training, especially during the first year of your pet's life, will be repaid many times over by giving you a well-behaved companion, one that is bound to you and your family for the rest of his life."

The corgi breed needs close relationships, something to keep them busy, and a job. The AKC says the corgi "without a job will often assign himself work, like herding children or his fellow dogs."

Millie the Weather Dog had found her perfect job. She excelled at that job. Ross Janssen says, "I'll never forget her employee evaluation for 2010. I think the only need for improvement was being at work more. She passed her evaluation with flying colors, came back with all perfect scores, and it's been fun to celebrate all the milestones with her along the way."[3]

Millie was appreciated by her coworkers for her unwavering love and positive outlook. Evening anchor Melissa Scheffler admired Millie's "supportive role. She encouraged me as a good cheerleader."[4]

Millie added her charisma to the newsroom. Janssen says, "I definitely think there's a lot of value to having a dog in the workplace, and she brightened the day for a lot of people."[5]

Good Morning America agrees. Dependent on an article by Janae Jones, one morning the show scrolled this timely ticker across the bottom of the screen: "Dogs at work can increase productivity and reduce stress."[6]

Millie's popularity showed up when the Kansas State Fair in Hutchinson rolled around each September. When she was there, she drew a crowd. When she wasn't, fairgoers asked, "Where's Millie?" News anchor Michael Schwanke remembers some lady coming to him at the fair and asking about Millie. Then she asked for the meteorologist's name. Schwanke needled Janssen about Millie being more popular than the meteorologist was.[7] Schwanke says, "We knew where we fell in the pecking order. Millie was always on top."[8]

Millie showed her love to children as she went with Ross on school visits. Ross remembers a time when Millie made a little girl's day. He says, "There was a little girl, not very old, who was diagnosed with cancer. And one of the things she wanted toward the end was to see Millie. To see her face light up, to think that it was my dog that would bring so much joy to somebody, that's pretty incredible."[9]

Millie is still greatly missed in Wichita. Millie the Weather Dog not only brought a smile to the little girl's face but was also the cause for bringing smiles to lots of viewers' faces. She impressed the entire city, as well as so many people in Kansas. Many residents loved Millie, and it was so hard to give her up. Thousands of television viewers appreciated Millie and Ross for their willingness to share so much of themselves in Wichita and throughout Kansas.

As we deal with the heartbreak of losing Lindsey and Millie, an old book published in 1942 comes to mind. Fred Gipson had been impressed by a true story his grandfather told that inspired Gipson to write the book *Old Yeller*. The book later morphed into a movie released on Christmas Day of 1957.

A teenage boy named Travis Coates has been left to watch over his family's farm because his father has gone on a cattle drive to Kansas to raise money for his destitute family. The family lives in Salt Licks, Texas, just after the Civil War. His father tempers his absence by promising Travis a horse when he returns. Travis's troubles begin when a stray dog chases a rabbit, spooking his mule to plow down a section of fence. Travis reacts by throwing rocks at the dog and threatening to shoot it.

Travis's younger brother, Arliss, wants to keep the dog and adopts him. Travis sets a trap for the dog, Old Yeller, by hanging a deer he has shot within reach of the dog and telling him not to touch it. The next morning, Travis sees the deer is untouched; the dog has refrained from taking a bite of the deer. Travis is touched by the dog's obedience. Old Yeller protects the family from snakes, raccoons, bears, wild hogs, wolves, and even the family's only milk cow, Red.

After Travis has grown to love Old Yeller, Burn Sanderson arrives at the farm to claim his dog. Once Sanderson realizes how much Old Yeller means to the family, he decides to leave the dog with the family, trading it for a home-cooked meal and Arliss's frog. A neighbor then leaves a puppy Old Yeller has sired for Arliss. Old Yeller is bitten by a wolf, acquires rabies, and becomes aggressive. Travis's mother totes a rifle in range of the dog, planning to shoot him, but Travis takes the rifle away from her. Travis has grown to love the dog.

After a long struggle with knowing he has to put the dog out of his suffering and belligerence, Travis shoots Old Yeller. Mr. Coates soon returns home with the promised horse for Travis, but Travis is depressed over Old Yeller's death and doesn't appreciate the horse.

His dad understands. He consoles Travis. His father says life can knock one down and cause pain. But we must look for the good among the bad. *Look for the good*. Travis doesn't want to accept his father's advice, but then he watches as the new puppy takes some venison in the same way Old Yeller did. He then smiles and realizes Dad's advice is true. Look for the good.

7
•••••

Sneaking into the Motel

The day came when we felt relieved that everything was packed, and we were loaded up to move to Wichita. We felt blessed that our church conference had contracted a moving company to move 95 percent of our possessions. But we still filled both of our cars with what we thought were our valuables. Peaches rode in my tightly packed car during the 140-mile trip from Coffeyville to Wichita. On a hot day in late June, the movers had loaded our belongings and would unload the next day.

The first night we had nowhere to stay except in a motel room. Today, many motels will allow pets to stay in house while they add on an extra fee. That, however, was not true in 2005 when we moved. I was anxious about how we might sneak Peaches past the front desk when we checked in. I decided to put Peaches in my duffle bag for that venture, telling her to keep quiet. She obeyed and did not make a peep. She did bark a few times once we got to the room, but not enough to raise the ire of any motel employee. We never left her alone in the room, and no one ever confronted us about her muted puppy bark. The motel stay was another close call.

The next day, she was underfoot, darting among all the movers with no major damage. Of course, we tried to position her out of the way of the movers before they ran over our dog.

Because of the Maltese in her, Peaches was feisty. As a young puppy, she was ornery and independent. At that time in her brief life, she didn't care to be told what to do. She would bite at my pants cuffs when I tried to walk.

Peaches gripped down on Glenda's pant cuffs as she walked across the room, a picture that remains vivid in my memory. Glenda dragged her along. Peaches clamped down with her teeth with no intention of letting go.

She loved to unfold the laundry when it was neatly stacked and ready to place in drawers. We folded the same load of laundry two and three times. She hid panties and socks under upholstered chairs, under beds, and all over the house.

It was her teasing fun to chew at the seat of my pants when I got out of the car. Peaches could move really fast when working on that little trick. Especially when I was sure I had moved fast enough to escape her hanging on, she still chomped down on my slacks. She was trying to teach me a lesson, implying, "Don't leave me. Don't forget about me."

She would find the carcass of an animal bigger than she was, hold it in her teeth, and bring it up to the house. Snakes, turtles, and frogs were not exempt from becoming the gifts she brought to the house. Neither size nor species scared her.

My brother David was caught off guard with a similar surprise from his dog. David and his wife, Cheryl, also kept their dog—named Ellie—behind a portable gate in their utility room doorway. Half Maltese and half Yorkshire terrier, Ellie had an easygoing and quiet disposition. Early on this particular evening, their daughter, Marci, was also in their home.

Ellie was let into the house from the fenced-in backyard, and David was sure she had a toy in her mouth. He yelled at Cheryl and Marci.

"Who let the dog out? She has a toy in her mouth," David inquired.

"Dad, that's no toy," Marci replied.

Ellie had something between her teeth, and Marci was right. She had gifted them with a dead squirrel.

In a similar episode, our family members were crossing a bridge with a small brook below. Peaches gave us a look that indicated her plans as clear as any flashing stop sign. She looked at Rachel, our daughter. She looked at Kevin, Rachel's husband. We should have given her the stop sign. The look in her eyes said, "I am going to jump."

Before any of us could stop her, she jumped into the water. Glenda pulled her out, and Peaches was covered with algae. She soon got a bath that she detested.

She was showing off the poodle in her with her dip in the water. Bruce Fogle, DVM, shares some history of the poodle. He writes, "By the Middle Ages, hunters in Europe had selectively bred dogs with thick, waterproof coats that could cope with waterlogged, marshy terrain, as well as retrieve game from rivers and lakes. These 'Water Dogges,' as they were then known in Britain, were later to be called Poodles, taken from the German verb, 'pudeln,' meaning to paddle or splash in water."[1] Poodles are known for an ability to excel as swimmers.

If only we had heard Fogle's advice before Peaches dived into the brook, we could have saved her from the bath she hated. He warns, "If you take your Poodle for a walk in the countryside, or near water, be prepared to clean a muddy, wet coat afterward."[2]

Our new home featured a wrought iron fence around the backyard. The bars were four inches apart, so it wasn't any problem for Peaches to go right through the space between them. Just behind the fence was a sidewalk that circled all the way around a lake. Lots of geese were usually grazing near the banks of the lake. Peaches would run through the fence and chase those geese; they would flap their wings and fly away. Those geese would have weighed three times what Peaches did. No fear. Even if another species is bigger than you are, no need to panic.

She also loved to see how much toilet paper she could unroll from its holder. "Thanks for leaving a pile of toilet paper below the holder. It might be needed soon," I said. Or at times she played another little game to show just how far she could string the toilet paper from its holder.

Through all her playful tricks, she heard an important word from me: "NO!" Yet below the surface, we laughed at her playfulness and persistence. We would later miss her play when she got older and it didn't happen as often.

One trick that she never grew out of was what she did to stuffed toys. When she received a squeaky stuffed animal for her birthday or Christmas, she attacked. She chewed diligently, and she usually found success quickly. Other times it took time, but she didn't quit chewing. She was extremely focused on that stuffed toy so that nothing distracted her. We would see an eye that was missing, hear the squeaking inside the toy, or be covered by the flying white stuffing from inside the toy.

Soon after we moved in, we made friends with ten-year-old Amanda and nine-year-old Ryan. This sister-and-brother act loved to chase Peaches, whether inside or outside the house. Peaches loved being chased too.

We had a cream-colored duster on the end of a stick Glenda bought that she used to dust the furniture and lights. Amanda and Ryan held the duster up next to Peaches. That duster looked like her twin. Ryan and Amanda laughed and laughed.

Both of our daughters moved home that first year we lived back in Wichita. Rachel had graduated from college and worked at a job in the Kansas City area. That job did not work out because her boss wasn't making enough to pay her.

Andrea had been attending a university and wasn't happy there. She moved back home to consider which college she would attend next. By the next fall, she was enrolled in a different college.

Both daughters were staying in the basement next to the storeroom where we kept Peaches. One morning, I was trying to be quiet enough to keep from waking them up while heading off for work; however, I wasn't silent enough. The girls overheard my words to Peaches. "Daddy has to go to work now, but I will miss you. I'll see you before supper when I get home from work. I love you."

Both Rachel and Andrea enjoyed giving me a hard time. "Dad, is that the same dog you didn't want?"

Peaches poses with her twin, the feather duster.

8

•• • ••

The Daily Walk

Soon after lunch every day, Peaches sounded off a one-bark alert. She might as well say it. "Let's get moving. What's the holdup?"

If I was in the master closet or the bathroom, she hunted me down. Her message was clear. "It's time for the daily walk. Let's get going!"

Peaches loved to take a walk with me. She wouldn't go with Glenda when I was not along either. Peaches usually recognized the signs that the walk was coming. Should I put my tennis shoes on, she thought it was a sure sign. She could be fooled; my plan may have been another task like checking the sprinkler system or going to the mailbox. The clincher arrived when I tore off a small plastic baggie colored red or green. She knew what those were for: to clean up after she took care of business.

Some of the dog experts have said that the Maltese breed has a lazy side. But I have never experienced Peaches to be lazy. When I have tried to help her into the car, she jumped in by herself. She climbed fifteen stairs every day, insisting that she could do it alone and didn't need my help. Her independence was more important to Peaches than slacking. Fortunately, she never needed to be prodded to get some exercise.

Peaches had a bounce to her step when we left for our walk. She started her walk as if she was racing on the interstate and ended it as if she was in a school zone. But she loved our walks.

Every day when there was no rain or snowstorm, Peaches went on a walk with me around our neighborhood. If there was a forty-mile-per-hour wind or bone-chilling cold, we went half the normal route.

The daily walk kept her regular. Glenda and I sent her out to poop numerous times a day. Once in a "super blood wolf moon," we got results. But Peaches always left her dog muck for me to pick up during a walk.

Peaches acted out many warning signals to help me know it was coming. She walked in baby steps, scanning the grass for the perfect spot to deliver her deposit. She took her time because it was so hard to find the ideal location to leave her poop behind. When she began to walk faster, she circled the most prominent place and then zeroed in on where her radar landed. Once she completed her meticulous search, she squatted.

She began to rock up and down with her back legs in a flawless imitation of a rocking chair. After she has completed the job, it was important to Peaches to sniff her handiwork and admire it. Then it was up to me to find all the damage and pick it up in the baggie I tied shut. This process was no fun when the wind was blowing forty miles an hour! Chasing baggies, paper towels, or her waste in a squall was no fun!

In the past, we had four different routes we walked in our neighborhood. Peaches was skilled at alternating the routes. She would never go the same route two days in a row and had an uncanny ability to lead in making sure we walked each route every fourth day.

One sunny day, we reached our turnaround point at a corner house. The lady living in that house drove into her driveway after bringing her kids home from school and caught Peaches marking in her yard.

The lady went ballistic, yelling about ruining her grass. She said she was calling the police. She let us know that she was taking pictures of us on her cell phone as we walked away. The kicker was that the way that yard looked, Peaches couldn't have killed anything but weeds. Peaches wasn't planning on being abused again, and she never made a move to go up that street again. She understood. I would not have allowed her to go up that street anyway, so we were thankful to have three routes to take.

Peaches was always up for a walk. She went into her spin cycle the minute she knew for sure that we were going. She had me well trained to go for a daily walk. When it was cold out, I put a sweater on her. With her heavy coat of fur, she handled the cold better than the heat.

When it was really hot, she plopped down in the shade under a tree or a parked vehicle. A house resident has never come out to move that vehicle, but I watched for a driver just in case. I waited for her to cool off and breathe without wheezing. Patience is a virtue. I bide my time so she can get some rest and relief from the heat. I understand better since I have suffered heatstroke.

I was riding on a week-long bicycle trip called Oklahoma Freewheel. When we rode out of Clayton at six thirty in the morning, the local bank posted a temperature of seventy-seven degrees. The humidity was high. We climbed up and coasted down the Ouachita Mountains that day. I was drinking lots of fluids yet still running low on energy. My condition may have been caused by my trying unsuccessfully to sleep on concrete in the open air at the fairgrounds the night before.

While slowing down my pace on the bike, I noticed a fellow biker lying in the ditch, ambulance close by. Other cyclists said he had heatstroke. Three miles from the end of that day's ride, I lost feeling in my right arm. My elbow was numb. I could not move my right hand. Still, determination was at the top of my list because I had never quit marathons or anything else. And I persisted in thinking, "Only three more miles." Yet I was at the end of my rope. When the SAG (support and gear) driver asked whether I needed a ride, my answer was a reluctant yes.

The next day, I was planning on riding again. But after looking at sausage and eggs, I couldn't eat. No ride that day. Hopefully, the next day. Again, I looked at breakfast and couldn't eat. I called Glenda, and she drove down to Pryor to pick me up. I had learned what heatstroke feels like. That experience made it a priority to protect Peaches from the heat.

Back when I was working lots of hours, Peaches and I would walk at five o'clock in the morning. I owned a flashlight that was made to fit on my bicycle. I recharged it every day and shined it on the sidewalk so we could see where we were going. It was bright enough to make other walkers shield their eyes. Neighbors complained about how bright that flashlight was. That flashlight got them up too early in the morning!

We were not living in a safe neighborhood. Houses and the church across from us were being robbed. One morning we were walking early while multiple police cars flashed red lights across the street from us. We learned a meth dealer was being busted, and his lab would be out of business.

Another morning, Peaches and I were walking in that neighborhood before sunrise. We were two blocks from home when we heard a harsh noise from across the street. "What are you doing?" a man in his seventies yelled gruffly. He sounded scary.

"Walking my dog," I said in my kindest voice.

Silence. Peaches didn't bark. We went on with our walk with no major problems. It could have been worse. That neighbor knew of the robberies in our neighborhood and felt the need to protect himself.

When we left for our walk, I loved watching her hop through the grass, bouncing like a Super Ball on a concrete driveway. Some days, my patience waned when she stopped at every driveway to mark and snoop at every blade of grass. When we returned home, Peaches drank lots of water. She taught us a thing or two about drinking plenty of water. I was amazed at how often her water dish needed to be filled.

The daily walk offered Peaches and me lots of benefits: exercise, fresh air, and the opportunity to meet some great people on the sidewalk, as well as humor, honesty, and teaching from young children.

Peaches and I enjoyed our daily walks, but she had a nephew who hated to walk. Roscoe was the dog owned by my kind niece, Abby. Roscoe, a cocker spaniel, went for walks with Abby but hated every step of the trip. He wasn't fond of jogging with Abby either. Whenever Abby put her jogging clothes on, Roscoe would fake a limp so he wouldn't have to go. If that didn't work, he would run to the kennel in hopes that that would save him from the walk or the jog. Roscoe is the exception to the American Kennel Club's take on cocker spaniels. It says, "These energetic sporting dogs love playtime and brisk walks."

The AKC says the cocker spaniel is "gentle, smart, and happy." It was one of the first nine breeds registered by the AKC in 1878 and recognized once the club was founded in 1884. Cocker spaniels are the "smallest member of the sporting-dog family."

The AKC adds this:

The merry and frolicsome Cocker Spaniel, with his big, dreamy eyes and impish personality, is one of the world's best loved breeds. They were developed as hunting dogs, but Cockers gained their wide popularity as all-around companions.

Those big, dark eyes; that sweet expression; those long, lush ears that practically demand to be touched—no wonder the Cocker spent years as America's most popular breed. The coat comes in enough colors and patterns to please any taste. The well-balanced body is sturdy and solid, and these quick, durable gun dogs move with a smooth, easy gait.

Cockers are eager playmates for kids and are easily trained as companions and athletes.

Roscoe's "impish" side showed up often, as he found trouble in a bundle of ways. He always discovered a new way to nose into the trash. Abby made flower arrangements for her cousin's wedding, but Roscoe got into the flowers and destroyed them all. Abby's only recourse was to start over with making flowers.

Once, Abby's mother, Ronda, went to Abby's house to find her crying in the driveway. Roscoe had torn into the Christmas packages and devastated the elegant wrapping paper. Abby had no choice but to wrap them over.

When Roscoe knew he was in trouble, he would climb up on top of the couch and then wink at Abby. His message was, "Don't blame me. Let's negotiate on this mischief."

Ronda and Abby have owned a number of other dogs who are an important part of their lives. Ronda always wanted a lapdog; Molly thought she was a lapdog, even though she was over two feet tall. Molly's breed included part English setter.

The AKC says the temperament of an English setter shows up "friendly, mellow, and merry." Like the cocker spaniel, the English setter was one of the first nine breeds recognized by the American Kennel Club. The AKC says, "English Setters were trained bird dogs in England more than 400 years ago." It continues like this:

> English Setters are elegant but solid dogs of beauty and charm. The word "belton," unique to the breed, describes the speckled coat patterns of colors that sound good enough to eat: liver, lemon, and orange among them. Under the showy coat is a well-balanced hunter standing about twenty-five inches at the shoulder.
>
> A graceful neck carries a long, oval-shaped head proudly, and dark brown eyes convey a soft expression. The merry English Setter is known as the gentleman of the dog world but is game and

boisterous at play. English Setters get on well with other dogs and people. A veteran all-breed handler says, "As a breed to share one's life and living space with, no other breed gives me more pleasure than the English Setter."

The English Setter is a medium-sized sporting dog of a sweet temper and show-stopping good looks. It is one of the AKC's four British setters created to work on the distinctly different terrains of England, Ireland, and Scotland.

Molly, representing the English Setter, loved to run with Abby. Molly ran every day with Abby; together they ran as far as ten miles during their jog. Molly would run by Ronda's old house and Ronda's deceased father's old house, go up to the respective door, and smell it. Later in her life, Molly got old and couldn't run a mile any more. Molly's heart ached with regret when she couldn't run with Abby any longer.

English setters have earned a reputation as adept hunting dogs. Ronda's husband, Larry, took Molly out hunting and shot the gun off. Immediately, Molly ran to the pickup, jumped in the window, got into the back seat, and shook all over in fear. Molly didn't care about an English setter's reputation as a good hunting dog!

Molly had a couple of routines she followed every night. After everyone was in bed and the lights had gone out, Molly went around to all the family members and checked to make sure they were doing all right. And she smelled everyone's breath. Just before she died, her last act was to smell everyone's breath. Ronda said, "She could have been a K-9 drug-sniffing dog."

Molly was nearly eighteen years old when she passed away.

Abby's current dog, Hosmer, is a cocker spaniel who loves to sing. His favorite is to sing along with Meghan Trainor on "All about That Bass." That song really winds Hosmer up.

Ronda and Abby currently own Cavalier King Charles spaniels named Charlie and Ruby. Both dogs have been quite loving to Abby's children: Ronnie, three years old, and Evie, two. Those Cavalier King Charles dogs have never growled at these little children.

The American Kennel Club says this:

The Cavalier King Charles Spaniel lives for love. You'd be hard pressed to find a sweeter, more affectionate dog or one who wants to please his or her person more than a Cavalier. Although due to their hunting-dog ancestry they love a good romp in the field, their even greater delight is simply to be with you.

Toy spaniels of similar type were the favorites of England's King Charles II in the seventeenth century, and reportedly he was rarely seen without two or three of the merry little dogs at his heels.

The breed standard describes the Cavalier as "gentle and affectionate" and says that the breed's characteristic happy temperament, "combined with true elegance and royal appearance," is of paramount importance.

With their silky coat in a tapestry of colors, soulful
eyes, and long, soft ears there are few dogs with
more charm and appeal than the graceful, devoted
Cavalier.

Ronda's Cavalier won't get off the porch until another of her
dogs, Tate, arrives as well. They snuggle together. Tate is half Jack
Russell terrier, half rat terrier. The Jack Russell terrier breed will be
described in chapter 11 ("Outfoxing Jack Russell"), and the rat terrier
will be portrayed in chapter 18 ("Manners Galore").

During the first week of May, we were deluged, showing an overflowing rain gauge in Wichita and nearby little towns. Douglass received over ten inches during one of the rainstorms. The turnpike
south out of Wichita closed down because of flooding. Schools and
homes were underwater, and as a result, there was no school for the
kids. Many bridges were out, and people tried to recover from the
flood.

We prayed for the many victims trying to recover, aware that we
dodged the torrent of water. Peaches knew it didn't affect her much,
except for what she thought was the awful news that she and I missed
out on our walk yesterday. How tragic to her!

I was writing away on my PC at eleven o'clock that morning,
focused on putting something meaningful into words. Peaches started barking. I was thinking, "You know our walk happens in the
afternoon."

I ignored her. Can't stop when I am on a roll. I was concentrating
on the writing before me.

Peaches couldn't live without her daily walk.

She persisted with her barking. I continued to play as if I did not hear. Her message to me was, "I missed the walk all day yesterday. I will not wait any longer."

I gave in. The writing would still be there when we arrived back home. Besides, I needed the exercise. Obviously, Peaches was convinced she did too. I went to the closet to find my running shoes.

The spec sheet on Maltese dogs says they are energetic and agile. Another comment is that they are high energy, so you will want to give them plenty of exercise to keep them happy. She has found happiness again. I wished we could all find as much happiness in exercise as Peaches did.

"Good job, little buddy," I said to her when we arrived home, while fishing out a treat from the box.

"You did good on our walk today! You did great!" I added, remembering that talking to her causes my intelligence to go up, and encouraging words help build a dog's self-esteem.

9

•• ● ••

Barking Chihuahuas

When a Chihuahua is mentioned, I immediately picture a yapping little dog. Chihuahuas are known for taking control. The American Kennel Club offers an apt description. It says, "Inside each little Chihuahua is a miniature king or queen ready to rule their realms, so they need to be taught what is acceptable in human kingdoms." Chihuahuas are intelligent, trainable, demanding, and low maintenance. They are able to connect with a family, especially if the children are able to be patient and gentle.

Even though we may remember them for their barking, they have many positive characteristics. Amanda Harding, writing for the American Kennel Club Culture Cheat Sheet, relates that Chihuahuas are rated number one of all breeds for adapting to people who work full time outside the home.[1] They are among those breeds that live the longest, often living to eighteen years old. The Chihuahua is one of the smallest dogs, normally weighing three to six pounds.

Surprisingly, Chihuahuas' barking can become a positive attribute, as they rate near the top as watchdogs.[2] How can a tiny Chihuahua qualify as a watchdog? A bigger dog might do a better job of scaring the opposition away. Granted, a Chihuahua is quite aggressive in protecting her territory; her bark would certainly keep a stranger from sneaking up on you. A Chihuahua's bark also has the potential to make enemies out of all the neighbors. Another jolting eye-opener is that the Chihuahua is one of only two small dogs included in a list titled "The 30 Most Dangerous Dogs," also known as "Dogs You Should Not Mess With."[3]

We had quite a few Chihuahuas over the years. The first dog I remember was a Chihuahua that Dad named Chico, a word meaning "boy, child, or kid" in Spanish. Chihuahuas originated in Mexico; the name of the breed is derived from the state of Chihuahua in Mexico.

Chico was white with dark brown ears and a dark brown spot on the right side of her body. Chico was very prolific during my days in elementary school, bearing at least four litters of itty-bitty puppies. Each litter consisted of five puppies, except for the last litter of six. One of those six was teetering on the edge of survival from the very beginning.

Dad fixed up his own homemade version of an incubator for the struggling pup. He placed her inside an empty corn bread box, heated her in the oven, and checked on her often. Due to his innovative compassion, she survived!

After Chico, we placed our hands over our ears for Taco, Poco, Tina, Lacey, and Gretchen, all Chihuahuas who were high strung and immensely vocal. When anyone rang the doorbell, the barking lasted for five minutes. It got annoying trying to stop the Chihuahuas from barking. Not that we didn't love them. In spite of their reputation for being dangerous, I don't remember any of our Chihuahuas biting anyone.

After owning Chihuahuas and growing up with them, I am glad Peaches is a dog who doesn't bark a lot. This is surprising, considering that the Maltese breed also has a reputation for barking too much. In

Australia, the breed most often dumped out on the street, deserted by its owner, is the Maltese. The reason given is the dog's excessive barking. The poodle in Peaches must have overruled the Maltese in this case.

There were times when Peaches kept quiet when another dog was barking at her. A huge mutt named Ranger who lived in our neighborhood was never the quiet type. Always barking. Peaches and I walked down the alley and right by Ranger. He growled, measured in decibels, trying to alert the neighborhood and protect his family. Peaches walked right along with me and never yapped. Her silence can be golden.

There are, however, times when she wasn't shy about making some noise. She intermittently revealed her ferocious side. On our walk, she ran up to a German shepherd behind a fence, and then both dogs started barking and running back and forth along the fence. The volume of the other dog barking competes with the rumble of a passing motorcycle. Peaches also barked loudly. I wondered who was winning the noise battle: the motorcycle, the German shepherd, or the Maltipoo? It was similar to football stadiums competing to see who can reach the highest decibel level. It was interesting that on our return trip, the German shepherd barked, but Peaches walked along quietly, pretending she heard nothing.

She could be pretty brave when a fence separated her from a big dog. She had a big bark with no bite. She acted tough but underneath was as soft as a pillow; a few people have been no different.

She communicated to us through her bark. Peaches barked to awaken me in the middle of the night if she needed a drink or to mark. The doorbell rang, and if Glenda and I were in the basement, neither one of us heard it. Peaches to the rescue. She barked to let us know. Should a stranger appear in our yard, her domain, she likewise barked. But she made friends pretty fast; she didn't forget if that person had been near our yard before. She barked when another dog, usually a much bigger dog, came sauntering down our sidewalk. It didn't matter how much that dog towered over her or whether it was on a leash with its owner. She was just protecting our turf.

But throughout a twenty-four-hour day, she was quieter than any other dog we've ever had. I am glad that Peaches was easygoing as well as pretty low maintenance. When she barked, she had a good reason for it. When she did not bark, maintaining her quiet demeanor, I enjoyed that her company whispered contentment.

Let us reflect on another painful memory with a Chihuahua. When Glenda and I got married, we both brought a dog into the marriage. Glenda had to learn to get along with Lindsey, my thirty-three-pound sheltie mentioned earlier. Lindsey would get immensely worked up and hyper when a storm came through. Thunder boomed. She paced.

Glenda had a Chihuahua named Gretchen who could bark loud enough to sound like thunder. We had been married a year when we moved to a new house. There we discovered a tiny room behind the enclosed garage that served as an ideal place to keep both dogs. This minuscule room, however, was not heated, so I connected a heat lamp above them.

Both dogs adjusted well to each other. A year later, Gretchen was thirteen years old. She was definitely showing her age. She moved at a slow pace, hardly walking, was nearly blind and deaf.

Glenda was working as a nurse on the evening shift at the hospital. I was in a "run to catch up" mode, late for a meeting and making a futile attempt to dress a one-year-old so I could drive her to the babysitter. After buckling Rachel into a seat belt, I backed my Buick out of the driveway. Before reaching the street, I heard a deafening thump. Had I backed into something? No, Gretchen had gotten out.

Oh no, I had run over her! I felt terrible! How senseless was that?

I picked Gretchen up in my arms and rushed her to the veterinarian. He didn't seem to share my grief. He nonchalantly said, "She's gone. There's nothing we can do."

At least he could have used a tiny bit of feeling in his voice. Even if he had given the same bad news a thousand times.

Then I had to go tell Glenda the bad news at the hospital. She had to work in the surgery unit and emergency room that evening until nearly midnight while grieving the death of her Chihuahua. By that time, I had forced myself to put Gretchen's body in a heavy trash sack on a high shelf in the garage. The next morning, I begrudgingly took a shovel to the backyard and dug a hole to bury Gretchen. The vet, a member of our church, had a bill in the mail the very next day for his ten-second service to pronounce her dead.

This whole sad scenario was never planned this way, but through God's grace, I saw His hand in all of it. Gretchen had come to the place in her life when there simply was no quality of life left for her. And the way details of her death unfolded, we were spared from the awful struggle of deciding when we would have her euthanized.

The question of life or death comes down to how much quality of life is left. In Gretchen's case, with her hearing and eyesight as good as gone, with her inability to walk well, the time had come when she had no quality of life left, and the more compassionate option pointed toward death.

Many times, I have talked with an elderly person who was honest enough to say, "I just want to die." Quality of life was gone. Many times, I have conducted a funeral for an elderly person, and the spouse has said, "I just want to go be with my husband." Often, it's not very long until she does. On the other hand, some elderly folk still cling to the fight to live, the struggle to keep breathing.

Answering three key questions can settle the dilemma of when to let the dog go on to a better place.

Is there no quality of life left for the dog? In Gretchen's case, the answer was no. I never would have planned it that way, but God knew a better plan. Have you noticed how "all things work together for good to those who love God" (Rom. 8:28)?

Is the dog in so much pain that life is no longer bearable? That was the situation for Lady with her stomach cancer. A time arrives when we cannot endure watching the dog in excruciating pain.

Is the dog too dangerous, too violent, to be around the family or owner? I have a relative who tried everything to keep her dachshund from biting. That dog kept biting in aggressive anger that was much more painful to the owner than just a tiny scratch. My family member slowly but finally made the difficult decision that the only answer was to put the dachshund down. We can try to make changes in the environment or eliminate triggers that set the dog off on a violent tangent. If that doesn't work, it's time to euthanize. I feel so reluctant to advise anyone to euthanize, but reality says the time will come when that appears to be the only alternative.

The other small dog that made the list of "The Thirty Most Dangerous Dogs" is the dachshund.[4] The American Kennel Club says dachshunds aren't big on exercise. It says, "Dachshunds aren't built for distance running, leaping, or strenuous swimming, but otherwise these tireless hounds are game for anything."

The AKC points out some important qualities about the dachshund breed. Their name is German for "badger dog;" because they are built low to the ground, they were able to go into badgers' holes in the ground and look for badgers. The AKC says, "Despite their small size, Dachshunds are brave and fierce."

The AKC highlights several interesting historical facts about dachshunds. The original, longer name for the hot dog was "dachshund sausage," so named because the hot dog resembles the breed's body. Wiener dogs were associated with Germany during World War I because Kaiser Wilhelm loved the breed, causing a decline of the dog's popularity in America. The dachshund was the first mascot of the Olympics in 1972 at Munich; the marathon was run in the shape of a dachshund that year. Until 2009, a wiener dog named Chanel held the record for living the longest of any dog. She passed away at twenty-one years of age.

That relative of mine who was forced to put her dog down had good reason to go through with it. Unfortunately, some owners euthanize a dog because the person is too busy to take care of it or for the owner's convenience. These are never valid reasons to end that dog's life. A caring family would love to adopt that dog at a shelter.

It would be wise and empathetic to refrain from judging those who have struggled over the difficult issues of whether to euthanize a dog or not and when to carry through with it. They don't need any extra guilt. We may never know all the particulars and reasons for coming to that decision. It's so hard to part with a pet, but don't allow guilt to weigh you down after making that choice. Accept the grief, never the guilt.

10

•••••

A Warm-Hearted Sidekick

Although Peaches became "my" dog, constantly following me from room to room, she overflowed with excitement, wagging her tail vigorously, when other members of the family showed up at our front door. When any member of the family came home, she went into the spin cycle, rapidly turning in circles.

When we are all together for Thanksgiving, Christmas, or Easter, Peaches was always excited about that. She was happy to receive her stuffed toy, looking ahead to chewing it up and pulling all the stuffing out with her teeth.

She usually chose to go with us to see our three-year-old grandson, Bentley, when given that opportunity nearly every evening. In the same way, when Rachel, Kevin, and Bentley stopped by our house, Peaches was all excited, wagging her tail and circling into the spin cycle.

With her nursing job seventy miles away, Glenda was gone from home for an entire four-day stretch. When I told Peaches that Momma would be coming home, she went to the door to the garage and waited for her. She heard the garage door open and barked. I opened the door and Peaches ran to meet Glenda, again wagging her tail in the spin cycle.

Maltipoos are known for wanting to fit in as part of the family. Dogs bred as poodles believe they already are members of the family.

Even though the poodle tends toward becoming very close to one member of the family, it wants to make friends with every member of the family. The Maltese breed is also outgoing, convinced that everyone it meets is a friend, and the dog works to foster those friendships.

Peaches was family oriented to the extent that she suffered from separation anxiety. The toy poodle, bred as a companion dog, is rated tenth among all breeds in suffering from separation anxiety. While the poodle captivates with a good-natured disposition, she desires love and attention from the family. One source listed the Maltese as one of four breeds that rate as having the least amount of separation anxiety. Another source said some Maltese dogs may suffer from separation anxiety.

Glenda and I traveled to Europe for ten days on two different occasions while Peaches stayed with Kevin, Rachel, and Bentley. Her separation anxiety dominated the first few days. She ate very little and cut back on taking care of business. When we finally got home, she was so excited to see us. She wanted to be held, she barked, and she acted out her spin cycle and raced around the yard. She was overjoyed that we were home. We felt the same way about her. We had missed her. The next few days after we got home, she made up for what she had stopped eating. She ate like the starving Akita breed and lapped down bowls of water.

The Maltese in Peaches made her demanding. The poodle showed up in ways she was picky. Don't touch her when she's eating, or she will growl. Don't move her basket when she is sleeping, or you will hear about it. Don't say the word *bath* out loud, or she will hide under the bed. We couldn't even spell it out because she knew what we were talking about. Around tiny children who didn't yet know to refrain from pulling her hair, Peaches snapped.

I once made the mistake of reaching under the bed to pull her out for a bath. She snapped at me, and I felt some pain, but her bite didn't break the skin. Peaches was not into hugs and sometimes moved her head to avoid a hug from me.

Yet with the passing of years, she has become more affectionate. She enjoyed lying on my lap and moved her head to make more contact with my legs. Poodles love to snuggle. It was just her way of communicating love. Her message was, "I care about you too." If she found herself in range of my hand, she started to lick it. She was giving me kisses. I reached down and gave her an audible kiss on the top of her head. She returned the favor, licking my hand. When she spotted a red sore on my leg, she made an effort to heal it by licking it over and over.

Glenda talked to Peaches with much more enthusiastic emotion than I did. She talked to Peaches with a high pitch, the way she talked to our eight-month-old granddaughter, Hartley. Yet her words to Peaches weren't baby talk. Glenda put her strong feelings into her conversation with Peaches, who responded by wagging her tail.

Once in a while, she wagged her tail for me but not nearly as often as for Glenda. Yet she always chose to be on my lap rather than Glenda's. Peaches warmed up to my love pats. She has also been very affectionate with Bentley, Kevin, and Rachel when we have gone to Europe.

She loved to lie on the blanket covering my legs. She felt warm and snuggly with another blanket over her. She was my excuse to procrastinate. I know I should be writing, but how can I disturb the warmth of a sleeping dog?

Peaches was thrilled to make new friends. Glenda and I hired a man to work on some construction projects in our house off and on. Jerry talked to Peaches, and she took to him immediately. That relationship led to another step when we asked him to feed Peaches and let her out during a time when we were out of town for the week. She fully trusted Jerry, just as we did. Peaches was willing to make friends with someone outside our family.

Glenda was once inside a department store shopping, and Peaches and I were outside in the summer heat. I am not big on shopping, but I felt the need to find some cool air for us. I entered the store, sat down on the bench just inside the door, and placed Peaches on my lap.

"Sir, we don't allow dogs inside the store," the saleslady said.

It was a clothing store, not a grocery store where a dog might get into food. I sat immobile and said not one word for once.

"Sir, we don't allow dogs inside the store," she said, in a much louder voice.

"I heard you the first time," I said glumly.

Defeated, not wanting to allow the car to idle in the heat, Peaches and I headed for the car to turn on some air-conditioning. She was well trained and would not be leaving any messes inside their store. They would have surely let us cool off in their store if we were buying all the clothes in the women's department.

When other shoppers passed by the car, I opened the window so Peaches could greet them. She wagged her tail, and they came closer and asked to pet her. "Of course," I replied.

Peaches always accepted strangers because she wanted to make new friends. She wanted to share quality time, whether with a friend or with a family member.

In like manner, Odin was a Great Pyrenees dog who loved his friends—goats and fawns—so much he rescued them from a roaring fire. The American Kennel Club describes the Great Pyrenees breed like this:

> The Great Pyrenees is a large, thickly coated, and immensely powerful working dog bred to deter sheep-stealing wolves and other predators on snowy mountaintops. Pyrs are mellow companions and vigilant guardians of home and family.
>
> Frequently described as "majestic," Pyrs are big, immensely strong mountain dogs standing as high as 32 inches at the shoulder and often tipping the scales at more than 100 pounds. These steadfast guardians usually exhibit a Zen-like calm, but they can quickly spring into action and move with grace and speed to meet a threat.

Exactly what Odin did.

Odin's rescue of his friends in Santa Rosa, California, was reported by Sarah Heise of KCRA, Channel 3, in Sacramento.[1] Roland Hendel and his daughter, Ariel, saw the spreading inferno and did their best to persuade their Great Pyrenees dog to evacuate along with them. Odin, however, refused to load up with them since the eight goats and the deer were not with him. Roland was forced to leave his farm, retreating with only a set of clothes, cell phone, dog, and cat. That fire was deadly, killing twenty-two people.

The fire was advancing at the rate of one hundred yards every three seconds, so Roland and Ariel had five minutes to evacuate. Roland knew they did not have the time to gather the goats. They loaded Odin's sister, Tessa, but Odin refused to go with them.

The next day, Hendel returned and found a "smoldering wasteland of our forest." He had lost his home, pump house, and workshop and the most special gift he had given his daughter, an all-terrain vehicle presented to Ariel for her twelfth birthday. She had used it to complete her forest chores.

Imagine his surprise when he saw the eight goats running to meet him. Odin followed, limping along with burned fur and singed whiskers.

Another problem confronted Roland Saturday morning when he couldn't find Odin or the goats. Hendel remained optimistic. "If Odin could keep them alive through the firestorm, surely they are alive and well now," said Hendel.

Hours later, Odin, Tessa, and the goats were found. Roland Hendel said, "Oh, blessed be. They are back. All of them. Safe and sound."

That evening, Odin was inspected by a volunteer veterinarian. Odin had suffered the burning of his paws and was still limping. The vet said Odin was in "remarkable health, given what he's been through."

Over $70,000 was donated to help the Hendels rebuild. Appearing on Steve Harvey's TV show, the family received a year's supply of dog food and $5,000. Roland Hendel wrote, "I am overwhelmed by the support that we have received from all of you. So much kindness and compassion. The human spirit is truly a remarkable and wondrous thing. Thank you all, from Odin and all of us."

Odin is an amazing hero who chose to risk his own life to save his friends. Odin spreads the love.

Another dog who was able to save lots of people was Balto, a Siberian husky from Anchorage, Alaska. In 1925, the community of Nome was undergoing an epidemic of diphtheria. The only antidote was 537 miles away in Anchorage. Balto covered the concluding leg of fifty-four miles in a blizzard with temperatures of forty below to relay the medication to Nome. For his efforts, Balto appeared in an animated movie in 1995 with Kevin Bacon voicing the dog. Balto has a statue in Central Park, and the taxidermy of Balto's body is on display in the Cleveland Museum of Natural History.

Let us focus on a group of trained dogs that show their love as "emotional support animals" (ESAs). They help people battling depression, anxiety, or posttraumatic stress disorder. The ESAs are often confused with service dogs who are trained to complete jobs for an owner who has an intellectual or physical dysfunction.

Carolyn Steber entitles her article in *Bustle*, "The 9 Best Dog Breeds for Emotional Support Animals." Some breeds that excel as ESAs are standard poodles, which connect closely with their owners; German shepherds, which offer protection to those dealing with anxiety but need to be trained away from being overly aggressive; Chihuahuas, which are small enough they can fit into any environment; and golden retrievers, which project an easygoing air of serenity.

Cavalier King Charles spaniels are gifted at helping people with depression or posttraumatic stress disorder. Labrador retrievers offer a tranquil air to those with attention deficit disorder or autism. Border collies are able to inspire their owners to jump into action, matching up well with those who feel depressed. Pembroke Welsh corgis sense their owners' emotions quickly and are always aware of their setting, assisting with those affected by paranoia. Not only do these ESA dogs help in healing disorders, but they also motivate their owners to serve others.[2]

Lauren McDevitt, cofounder of Good Dog, says, "They bring true friendship to the table, along with a sense of security, and at times, a great deal of stress relief."[3]

Another important group of dogs that serve are therapy dogs. They often care for people in institutions such as hospitals, nursing homes, hospice care centers, or psychiatric facilities. They too must be certified to carry out their loving care for the ill and needy. A test for certification weeds out dogs who are overly aggressive or vicious.

Aleita Downer of Cape-Able Canines in San Diego lists several traits the dog must show to be certified as a therapy dog.[4] They include being controllable, reliable, predictable, friendly, flexible, and patient. Therapy dogs must show a number of people skills. Certification requires the dog to display an outgoing nature, to want to engage with people. The dog must be able to respond to commands.

Downer says the successful therapy dog needs "good socialization—a calm demeanor, an ability to withstand loud, clanging noises and wailing sounds, as well as a calmness to ride in the car without getting sick."[5]

Therapy dogs put into practice the most important skill of simply showing love. Margaret Renkl published an opinion piece titled "What It Means to Be Loved by a Dog" in the *New York Times*.[6] She

compares the death of her Emma, a fifteen-year-old dachshund, with
the death of her mother, who owned the dog first. She felt a double
dose of grief. She says, "It might seem disrespectful to compare the
loss of even the dearest animal companion to the loss of a beloved
mother, but it makes a particular emotional sense."[7]

Granted, emotions overwhelm us when we grieve, whether for
a relative or for a loved pet. But it is not healthy to compare grief
for a pet against grief for a relative. Just as grief affects each person
differently, we need the space to grieve in our own unique ways for
each one, whether human or animal.

Renkl shares a couple of other touching quotes. She says, "You
can learn a lot about being a good person by belonging to a good
dog."[8] I feel extremely blessed by all Peaches has taught me as the
good dog to whom I belong.

Margaret Renkl sums up the love of a dog in the following heartwarming way. She says, "A dog loves a person the way people love
each other only while in the grip of new love: with intense, unwavering focus, attentive to every move the beloved makes, unaware of
imperfections, desiring little more than to be close, to be entwined,
to touch and touch and touch."[9]

Leslie Priggen lived out her love for dogs by taking in lots of strays.
Her story is found in the book *Second Chances: More Tales of Found Dogs*
by Elise Lufkin and Diana Walker. Actress Jamie Lee Curtis wrote the
foreword for this book, pleading for help and a home for "abandoned,
abused, mistreated" dogs.

Leslie Priggen grew up in England in a home where there were
dogs on nearly every chair, a practice she continued. When she moved
from New York City to the country, she had five dogs, but the number

soon increased to twelve. She found dogs in busy intersections. She found dogs that had moved more times than a migrant berry picker, more times than an itinerant preacher.

She stuck to one rule: no Jack Russell terriers. She felt they had been overbred and poorly bred in the United States. Then a desperate friend called to tell her about an aggressive Jack Russell at their house who had lived in four homes, causing destruction and gore. The friend's husband had endured a bloody fight with the dog; he ended up with a broken tooth and two broken toes. The husband was threatening to shoot it.

Priggen reconsidered her one rule and went to the friend's house to bring the dog home. She says, "He definitely had issues and more than a few bad habits. We had some serious lessons in the beginning, and now he'll do anything for me."[10]

She named the dog Friday, since she already had twelve dogs and this one had the personality to resemble Friday the thirteenth. Later on, she told the dog he would have a chance to be Good Friday. And that's how he turned out. Priggen later acquired a dog she named Maggie, whom she refers to as "a present from heaven, as they all have been."[11]

11

•••••

Outfoxing Jack Russell

My kid outsmarts anyone in her class. Many a parent has been convinced a child prodigy lights up the family, the community, the world. Of course, it's all in the genes. While pride may keep us from admitting it, we think about our dogs in the same way. Peaches hasn't read any bestsellers lately or studied thermodynamics, but she has displayed her intelligence in the following example.

Peaches and I were stepping off our usual afternoon walk. We had just passed the house three doors down the street from us. I failed to see the neighbor open the door and turn her dog loose. Out of the blue, Peaches suddenly raced off down the sidewalk, headed for our house. In hot pursuit was the much younger Jack Russell terrier our neighbor had opened the door for and released. Her dog was setting a speed record.

Peaches ran as fast as she could to avoid the terrier, but she knew she had no hope of outrunning the other dog. Peaches spotted our Camry in the driveway and ran under the car. And the terrier discovered he was too big to fit under the car. Peaches wasn't as fast as the other dog, but with her quick thinking, she had outsmarted him. She was also smart enough to include fear in her vocabulary.

This Jack Russell terrier and Tate (Ronda's dog) have earned a reputation for being "upbeat, lively, inquisitive and friendly," according to the AKC.

> The jaunty Russell Terrier was developed by England's "Sporting Parson" for use in foxhunts. The adorable Russell Terrier looks like a toy in a store that has come to life but is an eager, tireless working terrier.

> The jaunty little fellows pack lots of personality into a compact, rectangular body standing 10 to 12 inches at the shoulder. Their dark, almond-shaped eyes and mobile V-shaped ears bring out the keenly intelligent expression—an endearing hallmark of the breed. All three coat types are mostly white with markings that are tan or black or both. Russells move with a free, effortless gait that announces the breed's innate confidence.

That minuscule, running Jack Russell terrier definitely displayed its confidence.

One famous Jack Russell terrier starred as Wishbone in a PBS series that aired from 1995 to 1997. In the series, Wishbone lived with his owner, Joe Talbot, in the storybook town of Oakdale, Texas. He imagined himself as the main character in stories of classic literature, such as *The Hunchdog of Notre Dame*. Wishbone was tabbed "the little dog with a big imagination." Wishbone received numerous Emmys for his acting talent.

Another famous dog who hasn't been given enough credit for her intelligence is the cairn terrier actress in the movie *The Wizard of Oz*. Christened Toto in the movie, in real life she was named Terry. It's Toto who first figured out that the wizard was a fake. Toto's the one who pulled the curtain back to reveal the wizard's chicanery.

Dorothy and friends could not have followed the yellow brick road without Toto's guidance and companionship. Any dog in a movie must be commanded to act in the way wanted by the director and to carry out orders. Some dogs were gifted with that ability, and Toto was one of those who understood the director's wishes in a moment. Toto's memorial stands today in the Hollywood Forever Cemetery.

Poodle hybrids have earned the reputation for being highly intelligent. In many examples, the Maltese breed is also known for intelligence. Many times, Peaches has shown her intelligence. There were times when Peaches was too smart for me. She decided she needed some fresh air while I was driving, and she simply pushed the automatic button to lower the driver's window. She knew which button to push, and she had pushed my buttons. Quite annoying when I was driving down the interstate at seventy-nine miles per hour!

Her intelligence was immensely frustrating when my car is being pulled by the chain through the soapy car wash and unbeknownst to me, she has cracked another window. *Sir, I didn't ask for you to wash the interior, too.* I tried to push the right button to raise the window. I reached into the console for napkins to clean up the seats and dashboard. I was soaked. Peaches was soaked Oh, the joy of owning a smart dog!

She walked to her favorite spot beneath the washer. She knew her favorite treats were kept on the shelf above the washer. Then she shot me her best "give me" look with her puppy dog eyes. The subtle hint? "I'm ready for another treat." And I cave. Too often.

I caved too many times recently when she repeatedly went to the washer before bedtime. I kept giving her treats. Then she threw up. The next night, when she kept going to the washer, I said, "You get *one* tonight."

During breakfast, she camped under Glenda's stool and barked for a bite of donut. For some reason, she loved Glenda's donut more than my oatmeal. Duh. Other days, she liked Glenda's hot muffin better than my cold cereal. Duh. Peaches saved a deafening bark for Glenda's donut or ice cream but merely scratched at my pant leg for oatmeal or cold cereal.

When we went out for ice cream, I had to have chocolate in some form—rocky road or chocolate almond. Dogs don't eat chocolate; it's poison for them. Peaches got no ice cream from me, but Glenda never wanted chocolate. Therefore, Peaches got her ice cream from Glenda. Did I mention that Peaches had kidney stones and wasn't supposed to have table food? Neither Glenda nor I can escape confessing we were guilty. Yes, we gave her table food.

Just as she remembered every location where our daughters lived or worked, she never forgot a drive-through restaurant. As soon as we turned into the golden arches or the eatery that "has the meats," Peaches barked for french fries or ice cream. She recognized any eatery serving food.

Stanley Coren shared more results about which breeds are the most intelligent in his book *The Intelligence of Dogs: A Guide to the Thoughts, Emotions, and Inner Lives of Our Canine Companions.*[1] Border collies rated first, poodles were second.[2]

The dog experts have not recognized the Maltipoo as a breed but classified it as a designer dog because Maltipoos were bred on purpose as a combination of known breeds. It became a long, drawn-out process to become certified as a sole breed by the American Kennel Club, so as yet Maltipoos have not been officially considered a breed.

Peaches was smart enough to stay out of the street. Unlike some other dogs we've had, she comforted us because we knew she wouldn't venture too close to the traffic whizzing past our busy corner. We had to watch her if someone had thrown leftover pizza into the street. She didn't run away but occasionally felt the need to explore the three yards near us. There were coyotes in our neighborhood, so we didn't dare leave her out alone.

Her five-pound body weight dwarfed when compared to mine. She was smart enough to anticipate my next move and walk or jump out of the way.

She was bright enough to keep from taking care of business in the house. In cases when she has been very sick, it has happened. But more often, if it occurred, it was because Glenda or I got preoccupied with a household task and failed to let her out in a timely manner.

We have shut her in the utility room with the doors closed when making short trips, and to her credit, she has avoided going on the newspapers and waited until we arrived home. She could have read the newspapers but shows no interest in politics.

One of the most intelligent dogs who took up acting was Higgins, who played Benji in the movie by that name and was seen in 149 episodes of the TV show *Petticoat Junction*. Higgins was sixteen years old when he came out of retirement to star as Benji in the movie.

Higgins showed his intelligence with a wide range of expressions on his face, as well as the ability to sneeze or yawn on cue.

Higgins was a rescue dog, as he was brought home by animal trainer Frank Inn, who loved animals. Inn was convinced Higgins had miniature poodle, cocker spaniel, and schnauzer in his genes. Inn was a loyal friend to the dog and wrote a poem about him titled "The Little Brown Dog." Frank Inn rescued dogs who were listed on a shelter's calendar to be put down and made stars out of them.

Higgins worked a fourteen-year career in acting, including guest appearances on *Green Acres* with Eva Gabor and on *The Beverly Hillbillies*. In 1971, he starred in *Mooch Goes to Hollywood* along with Zsa Zsa Gabor and Vincent Price. Higgins appeared on the cover of *TV Guide* and received the award for Picture Animal Top Star of the Year (PATSY) in 1966.

Higgins must have understood hundreds of words with all his intelligence. The experts say a dog can understand fifty to one hundred words. Surely Higgins exceeded those numbers. Chase, a border collie, was trained by John Pilley to fetch 1,022 toys on command, as well as to understand numerous other commands.

Possibly because she was one-half poodle, rated number two in intelligence of all breeds, Peaches understood more words than a hundred. There were too many times when I told her what to do, and she complied immediately. I didn't have to tell her more than once. I told her something and it registered.

She wasn't faking me out, acting as if she knew what's been said when she didn't. She gave me a confused look when she didn't understand, but that didn't happen often. In her quiet way, she understood. I could not guess the number of words she actually understood, but it was more than one hundred. And she definitely understood the language of my love pats and kisses.

In our "two ships passing in the night" role, Glenda came home from work, unaware I have just let Peaches out to mark. She told Peaches, "It's time to let you out to potty."

Peaches gave her the look. She might as well have said it. "Really? Are you kidding me? You didn't know I just did that?"

Many times, Peaches said no with the expression she posed.

Peaches was clever enough to refrain from getting in too big a hurry. When she woke up and climbed the stairs, she waited at the bottom of the stairs, as if to say, "You first. You take care of what you need to do, and I'll bide my time until you can take care of me."

I had to say, "Come on, Peaches—let's go outside."

She loved to stop and smell the roses and a few other things. Lots of people could learn the art of slowing down. Life isn't all hurry and worry.

Peaches took on a mothering role at times. She had to know where the rest of the family was. If she didn't know where Glenda was in the house, she went from room to room to find her. She looked for me in the same way.

In terms of discerning dogs, guide dogs are brilliant in leading the blind. Two dogs who have shown quick thinking are Roselle and Salty, both guide dogs who brought their owners to safety after the World Trade Center towers were struck down by hijacked jets on September 11, 2001. Both dogs were awarded the Dickin Medal by a British charity, the People's Dispensary for Sick Animals.

Salty, a Labrador retriever and the lesser known of the two, was on the seventy-first floor of Tower One with owner Omar Rivera when the World Trade Center was hit by a hijacked plane. Rivera worked for the Port Authority of New York and New Jersey. Salty, along with Rivera's supervisor, Donna Enright, guided him down to safe ground. A coworker tried to help by taking over the lead, but Salty refused to leave Rivera's side.

Roselle, on the other hand, has been renowned for her role as a heroine in the book *Thunder Dog*, written by the dog's owner, Michael Hingson, and Susy Flory. The book's subtitle is not quite as brief: *The True Story of a Blind Man, His Guide Dog, and the Triumph of Trust at Ground Zero*.[3] The book is a riveting page-turner, both inspirational and educational.

Roselle, a yellow Labrador retriever, slept under a desk on the seventy-eighth floor of the north tower while her owner prepared for a routine training meeting. After the chaos exploded, Roselle soon led Michael and thirty other people down 1,463 stairs in stairwell B to safety. The elevator didn't work, and it took a little over an hour for their journey down to the ground. Roselle smelled their fear; the book says that a dog can smell fear through 200 million receptors inside its nose.[4]

Thunder Dog also emphasizes that the night before the plane was hijacked, Roselle trembled as a thunderstorm descended on New York City. In contrast, the unshakable calm Roselle showed the next day in leading thirty-one people to the ground floor was quite amazing. Just after they reached the ground, Tower Two collapsed. Hingson says, "While everyone ran in panic, Roselle remained totally focused on her job, while debris fell around us, and even hit us, Roselle stayed calm."[5]

Roselle guided Hingson to the subway, where they were able to help a woman who had been blinded by flying debris. After they got home, Roselle played with Linnie, the dog who served as Hingson's guide dog before her. Roselle was calm, as if nothing had happened.

Roselle was recognized posthumously as the American Hero Dog of 2011 by American Humane.

After 9/11, writer Michael Hingson left a lengthy career in high-tech computer sales to take a job as national public affairs director with Guide Dogs for the Blind. He says, "I trust Roselle with my life, every day. She trusts me to direct her."[6] Roselle served as his fifth guide dog.

Perhaps Michael's most valuable role in the book is to help us understand a little more about what it's like to be blind. He went blind as a newborn because of a medical procedure used to supply oxygen to premature infants. His parents taught him to be self-sufficient in every way, never using his blindness as an excuse to keep him from trying.

He writes of riding a neighbor girl's bicycle when he was six. Even though another neighbor called his parents to pressure them into barring Michael from the streets, they bought him a bike. Hingson tells of using echolocation to skateboard or mountain bike.

Hingson emphasizes that the unemployment rate for the blind is nearly 70 percent.

The faith of Michael's wife, Karen, is highlighted in *Thunder Dog*. After the north tower was hit, Michael instantly called Karen. She then prayed, "My heart beats hard and I feel fear. Please watch over Mike and the others in those towers. Lord, keep them safe and help them to make it out. Get Mike home safely."[7]

Her prayer was answered in a positive way. This book certainly speaks to the heart in an inspirational way.

Peaches wasn't the smartest dog in the world. That title went to a border collie. But Peaches was pretty intelligent. We may think we are intelligent, and we may think our children are smart, but none of us are too smart to learn a thing or two from a dog.

12

··●··

Kidney Stone Disaster

When Peaches was five years old, we let her out of the house to mark. No luck. Glenda and I watched her struggle with the simple chore. Nothing but dry runs for about a week.

After watching her suffer, we concluded that things weren't going to change. We booked an appointment with our veterinarian, who said kidney stones were causing the problem. She told us removing them would require surgery, and we brought Peaches in for her scheduled appointment for surgery on a Thursday.

The only times Peaches had seen this vet had been to receive her annual shots. She barked in fear. Previously, she had not as much as yelped when she got shots, but she knew this was different. We admitted we felt some fear and anxiety, too.

After taking Peaches in that Thursday afternoon, we were told to pick her up Friday evening. We said our prayers, went to work the next day, and showed up on time Friday, expecting Peaches to be sore and recovering but making progress toward healing.

The vet was not in, but her assistant brought Peaches to us. The first thing we saw was Peaches' glazed eyes and look of fear. Then we noticed that her insides were hanging out below her stomach where the incision had been made. Not a pretty picture, guts and all. The assistant explained that the glue they applied after surgery had not held her together.

"Can you do anything about it?" I asked.

"No, I am not licensed to perform surgery or do anything to put her back together," she replied.

"Can the vet do anything to put her back together?"

"No, she is at a wedding. She can't come in."

"Does she have another vet who is on call for her?"

"No."

We grimaced as we tried to process the news and Peaches' drastic condition. Not even another vet on call? Surely she wouldn't leave us hanging like this. Not only was our dog in serious, critical condition, about to die, but we were now abandoned and stranded by our vet. It was suddenly clear that the vet would not as much as take a call to talk to us.

Panic!

Where could we find help for our dog, who wouldn't last long in this condition? The assistant did mention that there was an animal hospital fifty miles away that might admit her. We called the hospital staff, afraid that they would not see us on a weekend. We explained our dilemma, and they said to bring her in.

It was nine o'clock on Friday evening when we arrived at the animal hospital and another hour before she was admitted. Peaches looked pretty scared. They told us they needed twenty-four hours with her.

"Come back at the same time tomorrow evening."

Neither Glenda nor I was able to sleep well that night. Seeing our dog with her insides hanging out was not something we had expected nor were we prepared for the bad news. The next day was much longer than usual. We prayed a lot, even asking God what we had done to deserve this and what we could have done differently.

When we arrived at the animal hospital, we found Peaches looking much more alert, even if she was not too fond of the cone she would have to wear for the next week. The hospital gave us medications for her pain. I wrote a check for over a thousand dollars, but we knew it was worth it to have her back on the road to recovery.

That was the last time that vet ever saw us. We found another veterinarian we liked who didn't abandon us when we needed help.

We were told that from that point on Peaches would have to eat only kidney-function dog food. No table food. The special diet food was more expensive, but we didn't mind buying the kidney-function food for her. The table food? Let's just say we worked at keeping it to a minimum.

Peaches wasn't the only dog suffering from kidney stones. Dogs of every breed suffer pain from kidney stones. Peter Dobias, DVM, says, "Tens of thousands of dogs suffer from urinary tract disease and stones."[1] The presence of the kidney stones is not usually recognized until the dog is in pain. The usual treatment cycles through the following pattern: a special diet, fluid therapy, hospitalization, catheterization, and surgery.

An elevated mineral content including high proportions of calcium, magnesium, and phosphorus is generally thought to be the cause. But Dr. Dobias says that the reason for the stones can also be a deficiency of calcium and other minerals.[2] He believes heavily processed food, including brewers rice, chicken byproduct, preserved pork fat, dried egg product, calcium sulfate, lactic acid, and chicken liver flavor, may be the cause.

Peta Owens-Liston works as a science communications writer for ARUP Laboratories in Salt Lake City, Utah. She has figured the average cost of the surgery to remove kidney stones from dogs is $3,500.[3] Pardon me for complaining about paying slightly above the $1,000 charge.

The cause of the kidney stones is crystal formations that result from a concentration of mineral salts in the dog's urine. It can lead to tissue damage and a urinary tract infection. The pain, Owens-Liston says, is worse than that of having a baby.[4] One man said, "It's like giving birth to a watermelon," even though he admitted he had no experience in doing that.

Dr. Blake Hamilton, MD, says that the problem occurs when the crystals grow larger, get stuck, and cause an obstruction. When that happens, stones become a problem and cause pain.[5] Exactly what happened to Peaches.

Nine years later, we can celebrate that Peaches was on the verge of death and still survived. That calls for a celebration found in a couple of passages of scripture from the book of Psalms. "Save me, O God, for the waters have come up to my neck...The Lord hears the needy and does not despise his captive people" (Ps. 68:1; 68:33). And "Blessed are those who have regard for the weak; the Lord delivers them in times of trouble" (Ps. 41:1).

13

•• • ••

She Minds Better Than My Kids

One gorgeous spring day, Glenda was digging soil near our house, preparing to plant flowers. Peaches was unleashed, enjoying the fresh air a few yards behind her. Glenda turned around to find Peaches was mimicking her, digging her own hole in the grass. Peaches' fur had morphed from cream colored to a dirty dark brown. After Peaches had shown she could follow the leader, she had to be washed down with a bath.

When we first acquired Peaches, she was Glenda's little buddy. That lasted a few years until some things began to change. I was the one walking Peaches at five in the morning. Glenda worked longer hours. Then we moved, and Glenda stayed at her job two hours away for four days at a time. Eventually, Peaches became my little buddy. She chose to follow me around. She chose to sit on my lap, spending less and less time with Glenda.

Maltese are known for being extremely teachable. It has not been an unbearable challenge to train Peaches. When we walk, people on the sidewalk are amazed at how well she minds.

"How do you control her without putting a leash on her? My dog would run away the first chance he got!"

"How do you keep her out of the street?"

We do have a leash law in our fine city. For safety's sake, I have put her on a leash at times. When it's a beautiful day and lots of people are walking their dogs, she is on a leash. When it's cold out and most people and their dogs stay inside, a leash is not necessary.

One beautiful day, Peaches and I were walking quietly on the sidewalk when I heard a man yelling at his dog. It was the same man who had a fence on each side of his house with a sign reading, "Beware of Dog." His pit bull had gotten loose through their garage and was racing our way. He and his son chased the pit bull, who headed straight for Peaches. It happened so fast that I didn't have time to pick her up before the pit bull arrived.

I had no option left but to pull her up to me by yanking on the leash. Otherwise, the pit bull might have had lunch. Trust me, I didn't want to hang the poor dog by her collar. The dog's owner and his son caught up to the pit bull soon after he got to us, apologized profusely, and took the dog home. Peaches never barked or showed any sign or sound of pain. Whew! That was too close. How grateful I was that Peaches was on a leash.

When Peaches was not on a leash and we met another dog that was being pulled along by someone with a leash, she didn't run. I simply picked her up. I held on to her until we were out of danger. Some days, I have been forced to shorten our walk if the weather was freezing cold or a hurricane-force wind was blowing. She turned around to hoof it on home, following my command.

Curious, Peaches has occasionally taken a step into a neighbor's garage. I would tell her no, and she would pause for a few seconds, wanting to stay, and then head my way. She must have been thinking,

But Dad, how can I do any exploring? There's probably something valuable to see in there.

Once, Peaches and I were on the sidewalk headed home. I saw our next-door neighbor get into his pickup, ready to back out of his drive. Fearing the worst, I gave Peaches the stop signal and said, "Stay," offering the neighbor the right of way to back out his driveway. He waited on us for a little while, gave up on waiting, and then backed out. Peaches didn't move until the neighbor was in the street.

The neighbor drove up, then stopped, rolled down his window, and said, "She minds better than my kids do."

The Bible tells us that obedience to God is an essential practice for the faithful Christian. The psalmist says, "You have laid down precepts that are to be fully obeyed" (119:4). Jesus said, "Anyone who loves me will obey my teaching" (John 14:23). John, the beloved disciple, writes, "And this is love: that we walk in obedience to His commands" (2 John 1:6).

One Wednesday afternoon, I had returned home after surgery to remove a ganglion cyst from my index finger. I had the impression recovery would be a piece of cake. But after a nerve block from the shoulder down, I was unable to move any part of my right arm. I originally kept my tee time for the next day, thinking I could still play golf. Then I realized it would be important to let the other golfers know there is no way for me to show up.

The splint was on my right hand, my dominant hand. With my right hand covered with a plastic sack, I raised it in the air to keep it dry as I showered. With soap in my left hand, I struggled to reach my shoulders and back. Then my handwriting was hardly legible as

I mentally thanked my former basketball coach for motivating us to use our off hands.

Peaches has seen the splint on my finger and the sling over my shoulder. She still gave me her "time for a walk" bark. I told her there would be no walk today. No more barking. I was amazed at how gracefully she accepted that. I thought she might fight it. She walked to my recliner and jumped up onto the blanket over me and lay down. No protest. She offered another sign that she was willing to obey.

God asked Abraham, the patriarch, to act on God's command to bring Isaac, his son, to be offered as a sacrifice (Gen. 22:1–18). Take a knife and kill your only son. No test could be any tougher to obey. No father could complete that challenging task easily, but Abraham obeyed. Abraham prepared wood to burn, tied his son up, and placed him on an altar. Abraham's act was an example of what God did for us by giving His only son as a sacrifice for our sins.

God rewarded Abraham's obedience by sending an angel to instruct Abraham to sacrifice a ram caught in the bushes nearby. God promised to bless Abraham and his many descendants who would "take possession of the cities of their enemies, and through your offspring all nations on earth will be blessed, because you have obeyed me" (Gen. 22:17–18).

I remember waking up from a dream at three in the morning. God seemed to be sending me a message that a young lady needed a note of encouragement. Right then, I wrote Peyton a note and mailed it that same day. I had no idea what she was going through at the time but learned that later from her mother.

Peyton was a six-foot-three-inch recent high school graduate who had basketball skills. She had been awarded a scholarship to a major college. Her college basketball team was traveling overseas to play during the summer. Unfortunately, she got injured seriously enough that she would not be able to make the trip. Peyton was so bummed that she would not be able to go on the trip for which she had been so excited. Her mother later got up to speak to a church group and told the crowd how much that note of encouragement had meant to her daughter. Obedience worked.

I see a lot of people wearing crosses around their necks. They may even be in church on Sundays. Are they going so far as to be obedient to God and Jesus? Obedience is the real test of our faith. My fear is that we know lots of folks who give lip service to following Christ but fail to obey His commands. I am, however, thankful for those who do.

14

•••••

Lacey's Life-Changing Scare

We lived across the street from a weed-infested field that morphed into a "field of dreams" when a newly built high school and its parking lot were constructed. In the other direction, a rolling hill ascended toward the cemetery. Fifth Street was a well-paved street, much too perfect for high school students to do some hot-rodding.

One beautiful, picture-perfect spring day, our Chihuahua, Lacey, was busy sniffing the grass near the retaining wall in our front yard. Looking for greener grass, she wandered out into the street, even though we yelled at her to come back. I was getting ready to go pick her up.

VROOM! Simultaneously, a high school student peeled out of the parking lot and came racing down Fifth Street. He thought he was Dale Earnhardt at Talladega or the Indianapolis 500. With engine racing, he sped up to fifty miles per hour. We again yelled at Lacey, to no avail. She couldn't hear us over the roar of the car's engine. The streaking hot rod did not slow down but speeded up even faster.

We held our breath as we watched the car go speeding over the exact spot where Lacey was in the street. We feared the worst. We braced our ears for the sound of a wounded, yelping dog. We were not able see Lacey but expected to see a sad sight. Her blood.

To our surprise, Lacey came running as fast as she could for the house. We breathed a sigh of relief. No yelping. No blood. No dead dog.

Glenda and I were sure we had left the back door latched tightly. The last time we had seen Lacey, she was running around the house toward the back door. When we got to the back door, she was nowhere in sight. We soon found her inside the house. But we could never figure out how Lacey got the back door unlatched to go inside. Her fear must have motivated her more than we imagined.

We were overjoyed that she came running out from under the car. She had to have been in the middle of the car, between the outside wheels. She was too close to have been on the far side of the car, outside its wheels.

We never again had a problem with Lacey running into the street after she was spooked by the racing wheels. She had learned her lesson, another lesson in obedience.

Some animals (and people) have to be scared into obedience. What we could not make Lacey do with our verbal directions she decided to do after her scare by the flying hot rod.

Although this is not my favorite memory, I had a teacher who worked at scaring us so all of us students would make a better effort to improve our English. When we failed to meet his lofty expectations, he yelled at us. He filled the blackboard with examples of punctuation and capitalization. He gave us daily, weekly, and monthly assignments to prepare us for college. He had spent several years in the US Navy and was a personnel trainer in the US Air Force.

My mother said, "That's the kind of teacher you may not appreciate now, but you will later on."

As usual, Mom was right. I am glad she could see the big picture, because I couldn't. But my grammar skills improved. If not for his influence, I might not be doing any writing today. Lots of his former students have told me about the hundreds of lessons they learned from him, even though he had to scare us into obedience.

I have watched some, but not all, college basketball coaches who employ the fear tactic. They are demonstrative, passionate, and sometimes threatening. They scare players into obedience.

Fear is intensely real for a dog who has been homeless. A homeless dog will often feel threatened in its search for food. That poor dog has wandered the streets, not knowing how or where to find food. Challenged by another dog who is after his food, he may be forced into a fight-or-flight situation. If he becomes a rescue dog, the fear he has of not finding food may make him more aggressive. Don't decide to move his dish of food while he is eating. This dog will be afraid his food is being taken away from him, his fear causing aggressive behavior.

Glenda and I know a kind lady who brought a miniature pony to our granddaughter's birthday party for the kids to ride. She has a business of raising animals, including goats and sheep that she brings to fairs and special occasions like citywide Easter egg hunts. She told us she does not take in rescue animals because of the high risk of their violent nature or tendency to run off.

All my memories of my grandfather feature a minister who was immensely loving and kind. Most everyone who knew him felt the same way. Lots of people have told me how they felt his love. He took me to the state fair, just the two of us, for my fifth birthday. He and my grandmother gave me my first bicycle for my sixth birthday. I remember people constantly coming and going at their house, people who always felt welcome.

Because of his career as a general superintendent of the Friends denomination, many a pastor had looked up to him. He had fostered close relationships with lots of pastors. But when the time came that he wanted to arrange details for his funeral, I was surprised that he chose me and a college dean to carry out the honor of officiating. Some of the pastors he had loved were not expecting that choice either.

When he chose where the service would be, he decided on the church where his father and brother were memorialized, a church outside the denomination he had served for nearly sixty years. It was the same denomination I had served for twenty-four years. Another surprise.

Grandpa was full of surprises. Some things he never told me would make a good book. Eventually, that book was published. In his book, he mentioned the financial depression of the thirties, when he worked as a pastor making fifteen dollars a month. That church got behind two months on paying his salary. Another church paid him a salary of $200 for an entire year. He writes, "Many of these dear people were in destitute situations." He was thankful God took care of the family during those trying years.

He served in Walsh, Colorado, during the Dirty Thirties while its residents congregated in the high school auditorium to keep from breathing the dust. Eight people died from dust pneumonia in a week's time. He was told by the doctor that unless he left for a new setting, he would be next. Their younger son, then six months old, needed to be moved out of that setting to survive. And they moved back to Kansas.

He had no patience for people who had problems with their nerves until he suffered his own nervous breakdown. Then he understood that most people don't realize the darkness and depression accompanying nerve disorders. Many days were distressing and difficult for him.

Grandpa suffered as he watched their older son battle epilepsy and the resulting seizures. He did not understand why, even from a faith standpoint. That young man passed away at the age of twenty-four; Grandpa wrote that his son's death was his worst experience of his lifetime.

He was always so upbeat, cracking jokes, loving people, and he never talked about the hard times. Without that book, I would have never known about his trials and sufferings.

Yet he appeared so different when he stepped into the pulpit. Quite the opposite. He had been an auctioneer for five years, crying farm sales. He talked so fast that everyone had to listen closely. Zip! Before you could reflect on his last sentence, he was on to the next one.

His training to preach occurred before microphones were in every church, so he was taught to project his voice. He never needed a microphone. Before an entire congregation, I once made the mistake of asking him if he wanted to use a microphone.

"Well, do I need it?" he bellowed, in a volume that surely could have been heard blocks away. I don't recall anyone ever saying he wasn't heard. He never had a problem with volume.

He paced back and forth across the platform like a caged tiger. No one was sleeping. People told me they were scared of his preaching. I was too.

He introduced many people to faith in Jesus Christ. I know my friend John Havens and many more who were saved because of his preaching are glad he was scary in the pulpit. The Holy Spirit was at work. Salvation may have occurred partially because many people were scared, though I certainly would not minimize the work of the Holy Spirit. That was the style of preaching in his day. It's definitely better than not bringing others to Christ at all.

Today, we hear a lot more about grace and love. I would prefer people come to Christ because they see He is reflected in the love they witness in other people's everyday lives. They come because they see the obedience and faithfulness of Christians. On the other hand, overly pushy, zealous Christians have scared people away.

Ponder a childhood memory of mine when I was scared into obedience. My family lived in Friendswood, a suburb of Houston, when I was four. Our family drove to an outing at the beach along the Gulf of Mexico. It was my great fun to throw seashells into the water. Even though Dad continually told me to stop, I defied his orders and refused to quit. Eventually, a seashell slipped from my hand, slicing across my wrist. To this day, I have a scar across my wrist reminding me of my disobedience. I was scared into obedience because of my disobedience. Just like Lacey.

Peaches, different from Lacey, has not been scared of much. She has never shown any sign of being afraid of thunder. In her later years, she showed fear when something unexpected surprised her—a sudden, quick movement by a human or the unanticipated sound of a construction truck unloading rock. But her fear usually didn't last long. Even the Fourth of July didn't faze her too much. She got nervous when firecrackers went off in rapid succession, sounding like the reports from an automatic rifle. But she was still following orders better than our neighbor's kids.

15

•• • ••

Always Buddies

I went downstairs to peruse posts on the computer. Peaches followed, making herself at home on the blankets over the recliner. I ascended upstairs to eat. Peaches was able to hear the refrigerator or microwave from anywhere in the house. She was right behind me. I descended the stairs and plopped down in a different recliner to watch some basketball. I warmed myself with the blankets on the recliner. Peaches was right there, turning circles in her spin cycle. I picked her up and put her on the blanket over my knees. Wherever I went, she was sure to trail me.

A lady brought a Maltipoo into the store where Glenda worked. She said, "I have had her about a year and got her as a rescue dog when she was seven. She is really clingy and doesn't let me out of her sight."

Her dog sounded a lot like another Maltipoo who followed me everywhere.

Mentally, my rebellious side spoke up. Can't I go anywhere without you behind me? I can find the refrigerator all by myself. I like to watch basketball in solitary peace and quiet.

But the grateful side countered. Thank you, Peaches, that you wanted to be with me. Your presence was really appreciated. She moved her head to rest on my leg, letting me know she cares.

We discover parallels in our relationship with God. In our rebellious state, we don't want God around. We have a need to remain independent. Thank you, God, for trying to communicate, but no, thank you, I don't need you. I can certainly do it myself.

Yet when we eventually reach the end of our rope, we find that truthfully, we cannot do it alone. We need a God who can guide us. We really do need Someone who desires to be with us at all times. God is waiting, longing for us to say yes.

Peaches has displayed her loyalty. She has been stuck in the minuscule utility room for an entire twenty-four-hour day and yet was overjoyed to see Glenda and me when we returned home. People didn't react the same way. Although our games with our grandson got physically rough—whether it's football, soccer, hockey, basketball, or baseball; we played them all—Peaches usually wanted to see Bentley and his parents.

She has been faithful in her acceptance of all members of the family. While Glenda was away for four days at a time with her job as a nurse, Peaches was there for me. We walked blocks during the noon hour each day. It's OK that she didn't want to let me out of her sight. Peaches has shown her devotion by never running far enough away that we couldn't find her. Her constant love has never wavered.

The prime example of loyalty was an Akita named Hachiko who was born in Odate, Japan, in 1923. The American Kennel Club says the Akita breed's temperament is "courageous, dignified, profoundly loyal." The AKC adds that Akitas are "muscular, double-coated dogs of ancient Japanese lineage," describing the Akita like this:

In their native land, they're venerated as family protectors and symbols of good health, happiness, and long life.

Akitas are burly, heavy-boned spitz-type dogs of imposing stature…Akitas are quiet, fastidious dogs. Wary of strangers and often intolerant of other animals, Akitas will gladly share their silly, affectionate side with family and friends. They thrive on human companionship. The large, independent-thinking Akita is hardwired for protecting those they love.

The Akita breed goes back two thousand years to the time these dogs first inhabited the main island of Japan. They came to Japan with the first hunters on the island. Martha Sherrill, in her book *Dog Man: An Uncommon Life on a Faraway Mountain*, describes the Akita's heritage and influence on the Japanese culture. "From the sixteenth to the nineteenth century, the warrior class, the samurai, were inspired by the dog's courage and rugged fighting spirit. For a particular type of samurai infantryman, an Akita dog was his teacher."[1]

They were first called Akitas in 1927 and were known for always finding their way home, even after being lost. Sherrill points out some of their strongest traits. "They have hearty appetites, eating as much as eight or nine pounds of food a day, great stamina, sharp hunting instincts, and a thick double coat of fur that's heavy enough to allow them to burrow deep in the snow and sleep there."[2]

During World War II, the Japanese ministry of education composed a song with words glorifying "Loyal Hachiko," a song sung by schoolchildren throughout the nation. The hidden, underlying message was to be loyal to the emperor. Akitas were also being annihilated to line the coats of military officers with the dogs' pelts. By the end of the war, only sixteen Akitas had survived. Two of them were owned by the "Dog Man," Morie Sawataishi, who didn't own a dog until he was thirty years old but raised many more on his mountain.

Helen Keller went on a ten-week speaking tour to Japan in 1937 and was touched by the story of Hachiko, whose loyalty was later memorialized in a movie. Keller wanted a dog from the Akita breed. She was gifted a dog named Kamikaze-go (translated "divine wind"). Keller and the dog met reporters in New York City because he was the first of his breed on American soil. After that dog died of distemper a few months later, Keller wrote about his heavenly qualities.

"If there was ever an angel in fur, it was Kamikaze. I know I shall never feel quite the same tenderness for any other pet. He is gentle, companionable, and trusty…an unfailing source of happiness. I never saw such devotion in a five-month-old puppy,"[3] penned Keller.

The Japanese government then sent her a dog from the same litter as Kami whom Keller named Go-Go. He showed a quiet confidence and shared a serene, attentive, and careful spirit. He didn't take long to understand that she was blind and never got in her way. Go-Go walked around Keller's house in Westport, Connecticut, without ever harming her antiques.

Helen Keller was influenced by Hachiko, who never gave up on meeting his master at the train station. The loyal dog waited at the train station every day when his master came home from work. After his owner, a professor at Tokyo University named Ueno Hidesaburo, passed away in 1925, Hachiko continued his practice of returning to the Shibuya train station where he had met his master after work each day.

Hachiko continued to return to the train station for the next nine years until he passed away in 1935. Dog lovers tried to adopt Hachiko and keep him in their home. He always ran away, ending up at the train station, waiting for his master. His loyalty never ceased. An Akita museum in Hachiko's town of birth, Odate, highlights this breed.

A movie of this story was produced in Japan in 1987.[4] It was called *Hachiko Monogatari*. In 2009 a reproduction of that movie titled *Hachi: A Dog's Tale* premiered in the United States, featuring an all-star cast.

It starred Richard Gere as Professor Parker Wilson. Gere also appeared in *Pretty Woman* and *Runaway Bride* and won a Golden Globe for his work in *Chicago*. He appeared in fifty-four movies.

Joan Allen played Parker Wilson's wife, Cate, in the movie. Allen was a three-time Academy Award winner as well as the recipient of a Tony award on Broadway. She appeared in thirty movies and twelve television shows.

Sarah Roemer played Parker and Cate's daughter, Andy. Roemer was a model and actress who was cast in fourteen movies and four TV shows.

Kevin DeCoste played Ronnie, who was Parker and Cate's grandson. DeCoste appeared in nine movies.

The actor who appeared in the most productions was Cary-Hiroyuki Tagawa, who played Ken in *Hachi*. Born in Azabu, Tokyo, Japan, he appeared in eighty-one movies, thirty-nine television shows, and three video games.

The Hachi movie was ninety-three minutes long. With a budget of $16 million, it grossed $46.7 million. This movie did a masterful job of showing the loyalty and faithfulness of the dog Hachi, teaching scores of people about loyalty.

An even greater example of loyalty and faithfulness comes from our God, who says, "Never will I leave you; never will I forsake you" (Heb. 13:5).

King David must have thought the following verse was really important. He sings, "The Lord Almighty is with us; the God of Jacob is our fortress" (Ps. 46:7). He thought it was so important he repeated the very same verse four verses later. This could have been the forerunner of contemporary music. I love contemporary music, but when we sing "holy" sixty-nine times in a song, it becomes a little tedious. While "holy" offers an important theme, most of us can understand the message before the sixty-ninth time we sing the word.

The prophet Jeremiah writes, "Because of the Lord's great love we are not consumed, for his compassions never fail. They are new every morning; great is your faithfulness" (Lam. 3:22–23).

It's thrilling to know that God is always is with us, that God never fails us. Just as God's faithfulness is a blessing, I give thanks that Peaches followed me wherever we went. I was fortunate that she was still with me, but her presence has been in jeopardy at times, as the following story relates.

It was a gorgeous day in May—lots of sunshine, temperature in the seventies—when Peaches and I set out for a walk about noon. It went well as we walked past an exterminator and his customer and greeted them. We were about three-fourths of the way home when I said hi to a young guy in his thirties who had just killed the gas on his lawn mower.

Suddenly, from inside his garage, a Doberman pinscher came running out, sneaking up on us from behind. Peaches was ninety-three years old in dog years, but I've never seen her run so fast. She ran really hard for three blocks, with the huge Doberman puppy in pursuit. Peaches would do well in the Senior Olympics. The big dog wasn't harming anyone, but it sure scared us both.

I finally got close enough to pick Peaches up. The Doberman was about thirty yards away. Finishers in the race were in this order: Peaches, then the Doberman, then me, then the young man. I headed for home and wasted no time stepping inside our garage and hitting the remote to close the garage door.

Then we watched from our deck as the Doberman decided to dive into the lake behind us for a swim. The dog played cat and mouse with his owner. He playfully approached the shore, then went back out for another swim. His owner kept begging and gesturing for the dog to come out of the water. Yet the dog just continued to play the game with his owner for twenty minutes.

Finally, the dog came out of the water, and his owner swatted the dog on his rear. Later, the young owner rang our doorbell and said he was sorry. Apology accepted. We viewed the most wonderful excitement in our neighborhood.

I was delighted that Peaches stuck with me through all that. It was a blessing that she was willing to share her loyalty. .

16

•• • ••

Food Hound

Peaches devoured her food with quite an appetite for a dog tipping the scales at five pounds. Whenever plastic rattled or a sack containing donuts was opened, she was front and center in a flash. She has seldom heard the sound of the refrigerator or the microwave opening without moving quickly toward one or the other. She loved her soft food, which the rest of the family was convinced smelled like slop. Her hard food? She wasn't quite as excited about it. Her motto was, "Don't ever miss a morsel of food."

I admit to learning that lesson at an early age. I was a senior in high school, training and competing in football and track after school. When the sports were over for the day, I headed home for supper and then on to work at a shoe store until nine. When time permitted, I did homework after arriving home from work.

I was also in a growth spurt. I must have eaten five thousand calories a day and still stayed skinny. In the school cafeteria, I begged for food off my friends' trays after I had wolfed down every crumb on my tray. I drove home during the break between school and sports and snarfed down any food I could find. My poor mother was buying ten gallons of milk a week to feed five hungry boys. We didn't hesitate when we heard that dinner was ready.

We used Peaches' appetite to our advantage when we tried to motivate her. If she didn't want to come in from outside, we simply rattled the box containing the doggy treats. Or we yelled out the brand name of the treats. And she came running. Admittedly, we have spoiled her with too many of them. But her mini snacks were only five calories.

Peaches was picky about the food she ate. She hated to eat alone; she wanted someone beside her. She wouldn't get near a potato chip, corn chip, or any vegetable except one. Like me, she loved fried yellow squash. She found ice cream or donuts to die for. Occasionally, Glenda or Rachel fed her dry food by hand, piece by piece. She ate better when they did that. I refused to feed her by hand, unless she hadn't eaten much for a while.

Since she couldn't stand to eat alone, I hung out a few feet away, close to her dish in the kitchen. She tested my patience while she took forever to eat. She first looked at her food for five minutes on the nights she slowly munched on dry food. On the alternating nights when she attacked the soft food, it was gone in ten seconds. She dragged out eating the dry food by taking one piece at a time to the bedroom carpet. It surely tasted better there compared to when she consumed it from her dish.

Did I mention the one fruit of the Spirit I have the most trouble practicing is patience? God surely offers me a test at every dry feeding to help me grow in that fruit of the Spirit. I could find something else to do, but that wouldn't help me grow in patience.

One Sunday, her appetite got her in trouble. Glenda was working at the nursing home, and I came home right after church to find gold foil from dark chocolate on the floor below where I kept the chocolate high on a shelf. Somehow the dark chocolate had fallen off the shelf—no way Peaches could reach it—and she had herself a feast on that scrumptious treat.

Dark chocolate is like poison to dogs. I called our vet, Clinton Skaggs, the one we liked after the other one abandoned us, and he said to pour hydrogen peroxide down her throat. That procedure would make her throw up. He didn't even bill me.

I drove Peaches to the nursing home and interrupted Glenda's busy schedule. She gave Peaches the chemical, and Peaches did indeed vomit it all up. Another close call! It could have been worse if I hadn't gotten home soon after Peaches had gulped down the chocolate.

On the other hand, Peaches" appetite was a blessing. When any dog stops eating, there is almost always a serious problem. It's often connected to some kind of disease. It could be parvo, other infections, liver problems, kidney failure, or cancer. It could be an issue related to her teeth: a broken or loose tooth, inflammation of the gums, or an oral tumor.

Granted, loss of appetite could stem from the dog simply being picky. Going into new, unfamiliar surroundings because of a move or travel issues can decrease the dog's appetite.

A dog will eat anything. It's important to guard against any dog getting to nuts, chocolate, or any fat from meat.

I did my best to keep Peaches from eating anything in the grass as we walked. She snooped around some items she shouldn't have eaten; I told her no. Unfortunately, sometimes I haven't been quick enough on the draw. She has swallowed before I got her stopped. She has become ill from snarfing down a threatening object. I am convinced that Lady Luck's stomach cancer was a result of eating something outdoors that caused the disease.

"You are feeding the dog too much," Glenda said repeatedly.

"That's not a problem. Her appetite is a good thing. It would be a lot worse if she didn't have an appetite," I responded. "She's not getting fat. She stops eating when she's full. There's still food left in her dish."

Thank God that she still had an appetite at ninety-nine years old in doggy years.

Consider a true story about a dog whose loyalty to his master was much more important than his need for food and water. Canelo was the dog of an anonymous man who lived in Cadiz in southwest Spain.[1] The lonely owner lived alone, so the dog and man went everywhere together.

Canelo was from the Spanish dog breed called the Perro de Presa Canario, or Presa Canario. The breed can also be called the Canarian catch dog, Canary dog, or Canary mastiff. As you know by now, this dog's breed originated in the Canary Islands. *Canelo* is Spanish for cinnamon, so his name may have come from his coloring.

Each morning, the man and Canelo walked through the streets of Cadiz. One day each week, their walk would come to a stopping place at the Puerta del Mar Hospital, where the man was receiving dialysis for his failing kidneys.

Canelo was forced to wait at the door of the hospital because dogs were not allowed inside. After his treatment, the man met Canelo at the door, and together they headed home. This pattern took place for an extended period of nearly two years.

The day came when the man passed away in the hospital. Always loyal, always faithful, Canelo waited for his master. He could not understand why his friend did not show up. Yet he waited.

Neither hunger nor thirst would convince Canelo to leave that hospital door. Day in and day out, he waited through rain, cold, wind, or sun. He kept believing his friend would come through that door and take him home.

The townspeople understood the need to care for the dog, and they took turns bringing him food and water. They treated him as if he were a member of their own families. They went so far as to acquire a pardon when the local pound unexpectedly picked him up, planning to euthanize him. Agaden (the association for the defense and study of nature) embraced him, got him vaccinated, and acquired papers to keep him from being on the short list of the dog pound as a stray.

For twelve years, Canelo waited for his anonymous companion outside the hospital. He had no desire to be included in a foster family. Over and over, foster families would take him in to their homes. Every time he would escape and end up back at the hospital door.

His patience and dedication came to an end when he was run over and killed outside the hospital on December 9, 2002. He set an incredible standard of loyalty and unwavering love.

Members of the Cadiz community were aware of the example Canelo had set, and they honored his loyalty and memory by naming an alley after him and posting a plaque in his honor for all to see. Survival by taking in food and water was not his first priority; waiting for his deceased master was.

Canelo exemplified a meaningful lesson in how to show loyalty and unconditional love.

The Bible says, "The eyes of all look to you [God], and you give them their food at the proper time. You open your hand and satisfy the desires of every living thing" (Ps. 145:15–16).

17

•• • ••

Her Sense of Smell

Closely related to Peaches' appetite was her sense of smell. Peaches scratched at the door to the glove compartment in my Camry. She smelled the treat I have hidden there for her, even though I wasn't able to smell it. It drove her crazy; she would not give up. It drove me crazy. It was quite frustrating to me that I wasn't successful in hiding her treat.

I accidently dropped one of her treats, and it fell underneath the washer. She placed her nose next to the washer. When that didn't work, she started scratching at the floor. Again, it was making her out of control. I couldn't smell a thing.

When Peaches stopped to sniff another dog's waste, it was her way of recognizing that other dog. It may or may not have been a friend or acquaintance.

Dogs can innately recognize human beings or other animals by their smell. Smell originates in a much higher dimension and intensity with which all dogs are blessed and which are simply not a part of a person's arsenal.

A dog's sense of smell is way beyond what we humans can sense with our olfactory capacities. Even though an earlier study, quoted in *Thunder Dog*, said a dog has two hundred million receptors in its nose, a later study has estimated that figure at three hundred million.[1]

Humans have six million receptors. The area of a dog's brain that analyzes smell is fifty times greater than in the human's brain.

A dog's nose works differently than ours does in that a dog has one nostril with which to breathe while the other nostril is able to smell amazingly well. If a dog were to smell a pizza, it would be able to smell each ingredient (crust, sauce, cheese, and toppings) rather than just one smell as we do.

The experts estimate that a dog's sense of smell is ten thousand to one hundred thousand times as acute as ours.[2] That seems like such a wide margin. Scientific studies look for a smaller range upon which to focus. During one study, James Walker, former director of the Sensory Research Center at Florida State University, and some of his colleagues came up with the following illustration. "If you make the analogy to vision, what you and I can see at a third of a mile, a dog could see more than three thousand miles away and still see as well,"[3] Walker says.

One example was a drug-sniffing dog who smelled a plastic container packed with thirty-five pounds of marijuana submerged in gasoline inside a gas tank. The lawbreaker must have thought his device foolproof—only a dog could have found the incriminating evidence.

A stray black Lab from off the streets of Seattle was able to recognize orca feces as far as a mile away across the turbulent waves of Puget Sound.

One cancer-sniffing dog showed it was convinced there was a melanoma on a patient's skin. Doctors had already proclaimed the patient cancer-free. A later biopsy proved the dog correct in its diagnosis.

Some heartwarming news out of Junction City, Kansas, tells of an abused German shepherd named Nova.[4] The dog was brought to a shelter with a deep wound around her muzzle that pointed to the strong possibility she had been bound with a rope or wire. The Geary County Sheriff's Department rescued her with a plan of making her a drug-sniffing K-9 dog. After training, Nova was able to be certified in narcotics detection and tracking by the Heart of America Police Dog Association.

Her handler, Lieutenant Justin Stopper, was so proud of Nova. He said, "We thought we could provide a tool for the county that somebody discarded. And it was at no cost to the taxpayers," Stopper told the Topeka ABC television station. "Even her adoption fee to cover veterinary care was provided by an anonymous donation. It was very rewarding for me personally."[5]

It is quite impressive that this formerly abused German shepherd was employing her nose for a great cause. Nova has found a new home where she wcan receive lots of loving care as she goes about her important job.

Nova falls into the category of a detection dog (or sniffer dog) that is trained to use its sense of smell to find a targeted object. The dog searches for only one of several potential targets, including a wide range of items: illegal drugs, explosives, money, blood, wildlife scat, pornography, cancer, or an illegal cell phone in a correctional facility. German shepherds and beagles have the most heightened senses of smell and greatest ability to complete the mission.

A detection dog must become certified after two to three months of intensive training, the time dependent upon how well the dog responds. When the dog finds the targeted object, it is rewarded by playing tug-of-war with a towel. The sniffer dog learns to focus on that one smell above all others and uses its gift to block out any other smell.

Dogs like Nova tend to receive deserved acclaim from the media for the jobs they do, but roadblocks often slow down progress. Law enforcement can pay up to $11,000 for a prize dog and another $11,000 for its training. The dogs tend to burn out and lose their effectiveness within six to eight years.

A sheriff's officer told me about a fellow officer's episode. This lawman felt it best to leave the K-9 drug-sniffing dog in the car while he served a warrant. The officer was gone longer than expected; when he returned to the car, he discovered the dog had thrown a fit and ripped the interior of the car to pieces. The dog was a German shepherd, whose rank for separation anxiety is fifth highest among all breeds. This drug-sniffing dog had a message for his handler. "I will find a way to make you wish you hadn't left me alone."

Porn-sniffing dogs are trained to smell hidden memory cards, hard drives, and other devices. A dog named Bear found a hidden flash drive humans could not find. It had been hidden by Jared Fogle, who appeared in Subway commercials.

Nova morphed from a rescue dog to a drug-sniffing canine. There seems to be some stigma holding people back from adopting rescue dogs, but they have proved a good fit with many families. Their supply is plentiful. The sad news is that we have no way of knowing which rescue dogs in a shelter are about to be put down. If a lady shopping for a dog at a shelter knows the dog won't live past tomorrow, a change of heart could easily convince her to take the dog home. If no one picks a rescue dog out to adopt, it may not live another day. Although they are a risk, rescue dogs can make great pets.

It was a rescue dog who was the first living creature to orbit the earth. During the space race with the Soviet Union in the fifties, a stray dog named Laika was found on the streets of Moscow. The Soviets fired Laika up into space in the capsule of Sputnik II in 1957. Unfortunately, Laika lived only five hours while in space.

One morning, I took Peaches with me into a massive big-box chain store to buy brush cleaner for a project: staining the deck at home. The lady in charge of the stain and paint section kindly ushered me to the exact shelf where the brush cleaner was displayed. We began talking about dogs, and she unfolded an interesting story about her dog.

In the plant where she was formerly employed, she saw this dog each day down by a lake. For an entire week, she asked her husband whether they could take the dog home. Finally, he gave in.

She checked with the veterinarian and learned there was no microchip for the dog. She went ahead and paid for shots for the dog. The vet told her the dog was a mix between a black Labrador and the Chesapeake Bay retriever breed. She said, "That dog is the best dog." Except for one incident. The dog, weighing in at 125 pounds, accidently knocked the saleslady down once, resulting in a trip to the emergency room. While her dog wasn't an official rescue dog coming from a shelter, she and her husband certainly did rescue it.

An important question to ask is just how violent a rescue dog has been in the past. Samantha Bubar, in an article titled "Common Issues with Rescue Dogs," says that some shelters do test their dogs for aggression. She also says the rescue dog will test the owner's patience. Bubar says, "With love and lots of patience and training, you'll have a loyal, loving new member of your family."[6]

On the other hand, according to veterinarian Teri Ann Oursler, many shelters work under the false premise that every dog, no matter how aggressive, deserves to be in a home.[7] She cites numerous examples of the damage with which violent rescue dogs have attacked. One child was bitten in the face three days after her family adopted a dog. A Tennessee man was killed by a dog three days after he adopted it from a shelter. Oursler says, "Unfortunately, there are many shelters who do not evaluate dogs before placing them up for adoption."[8]

Oursler also gives examples of times veterinarians told a shelter not to put a dog up for adoption because of its aggressive nature, and the shelter put the dog up for adoption anyway. Beware of a dog who has been violent; perhaps placing it in a shelter was easier for the owner than euthanizing it.

While there may be dogs among the following breeds that are not violent, those listed below scare insurance companies, according to the United Policy Holders: Akita, Alaskan malamute, Chow Chow, Doberman pinscher, German shepherd, pit bull, Rottweiler, Siberian husky, and wolf hybrid.

Susan Kahler of the American Veterinary Medical Association quotes Dr. Janet Scarlett, the board chair of the National Council on Pet Population, on this issue. Scarlett says, "We want to put out behaviorally healthy, safe animals, but we also want to provide for their enrichment."[9]

The following statistics are not intended to scare anyone, but they point out the problem our society has with dog bites. How easy it would be to look the other way, deny the problem, and wish it weren't real. According to the US Centers for Disease Control and Prevention, 4.7 million people are bitten by dogs each year; eight hundred thousand persons are admitted for medical care. Cost for these medical bills? $675,000,000.

More than half of these dog bite injuries are to children, who are the most vulnerable to suffering severe wounds. Children between five and nine years old are the most common victims.

While Glenda was working as a nurse in the emergency room at a hospital, a four-year-old girl was brought in covered with deep wounds all over her face. She had been attacked by a Rottweiler. Glenda assisted as the doctor sewed the little girl up with 256 stitches. The doctor did not sew all the stitches on the surface of her face. Some of the stitches had to be sewn where the wounds went the deepest, below the surface of her skin. When the little girl healed up, scars were not visible. Her looks for her lifetime were spared because the doctor knew how to use this special technique.

Between 1992 and 2012, there were 238 people who died from dog bites. About twenty-five different breeds caused these deaths, with pit bulls and Rottweilers responsible for over half of them. During the period from 1982 through 2012, fatalities due to dog bites increased at a rate of 82 percent.

In an article written by Maia Belay of Fox 8 News in Cleveland, she interviews Dr. Tim Lee of the children's emergency room in Akron, Ohio. Dr. Lee says, "For smaller children, the face puts them right at the dog's level."[10]

Lee also observes that the most common attacking dogs are male, dogs that are not neutered or spayed, dogs that have been chained up, or dogs that have been left free to prowl with no restraints or human supervision.

Consider some dogs that accomplish things with their sense of smell that humans cannot. These are search and rescue dogs who have been through specialized training to help people in so many ways. The training can last from a year and a half to two years. The dog must be certified to be able to perform the job; its handler is also required to be certified.

Zori is a search and rescue dog who serves alongside her owner, Susan Read, as they volunteer to help law enforcement find missing people in Ontario. Zori is a Belgian Malinois, a breed often employed as a search and rescue dog. The AKC says, "The smart, confident, and versatile Belgian Malinois is a world-class worker who forges an unbreakable bond with his human partner. To deny a Mal activity and the pleasure of your company is to deprive him of his very reasons for being."

The AKC continues like this:

> Belgian Malinois are squarely built, proud, and alert herders standing 22 to 26 inches. Strong and well-muscled, but more elegant than bulky, there's an honest, no-frills look about them, as befit dogs built to work hard for their feed.

> If you have ever seen a Mal perform an obedience routine, you know firsthand what a smart and eager breed this is. Problems set in, though, when this people-oriented dog is underemployed and neglected. Exercise, and plenty of it, preferably side by side with their adored owner, is key to Mal happiness.

Breeds that excel at search and rescue include Malinois, German shepherds, and Labrador retrievers. Traits required include the ability to navigate all types of ground, endurance for journeying a long way, work ethic, the ability to center in on the goal, calmness to deal with obstructions, prey drive, hunt drive, and play drive.

Handler Susan Read says, "These dogs need to be socialized early on in age."[11]

Training begins as a game when they are puppies, progresses to rewards, and enlarges to games with particular job skills. The goal of early training is to teach the dog to sniff a person's odor and follow it. Bacteria on our skin cells create an odor and gases that the dog is trained to detect, and the dog receives a reward for tracking human skin cells.

The search and rescue dogs must be trained to let the handler know they have found the human odor. As the training moves forward, the degree of difficulty increases, so the dog learns to deal with such challenges as various temperatures, humidity, and light.

To reach certification, the search and rescue dog must demonstrate skills in four areas: obedience, agility, search, and tracking. The handler also requires certification in the areas of ground search, first aid, CPR, and other skills.

Amanda Littlejohn distinguishes between the different tasks of search and rescue in which dogs are asked to specialize. The air-scent dog simply follows the human smell in the air. The trailing dog follows the scent of a human after a sniff of its clothing. The tracking dog follows tracks and footprints. The disaster dog locates people after an earthquake or bombing. The cadaver dog, also known as a human remains detection dog, is trained to detect the smell of a human corpse, should someone be missing. The water-search dog works with a human team in a boat or along the shoreline to pick up underwater gases. The avalanche dog can detect the scent of a human under fifteen feet of snow.[12]

Danielle Garrand of CBS News writes about a disaster dog who brought hope to the people of Mexico after an earthquake of magnitude 7.1 on the Richter scale.[13] Frida, a yellow Labrador retriever, located forty-one bodies and saved twelve victims after the earthquake struck Mexico City and surrounding areas on September 19, 2017. Almost four hundred people died in the tremor, 228 of them from Mexico City. After Frida became famous, actor Chris Evans tweeted, "What did we do to deserve dogs?"

Frida also helped out after earthquakes in Ecuador and Haiti. According to Agence France-Presse (AFP), Deputy Naval Minister Eduardo Redondo said, "Frida stole the heart of all Mexico and thousands more abroad…Her bark always gave hope, and in moments of pain and uncertainty she brought relief. Frida, mission accomplished, with honor."[14]

At the age of ten, Frida has retired from her disaster dog role. But her heroism will not be forgotten. Remezcla reported that a statue of Frida was made public at an environmental park in Puebla City. Beside her statue stands another sculpture of her trainer, Israel Arauz. A plaque in front of these two statues reads, "Memorable symbols of the strength Mexicans can have when we decide to come together for great causes."[15]

As we took the usual afternoon walk, Peaches found lots of places to stop and sniff. The base of a telephone pole. The bottom stand of a street sign. The grass. The fire hydrant. The trunk of a tree. The metal base holding up a park bench. Of course, she was looking for an old friend with her overpowering sense of smell.

On a beautiful spring day, Peaches took time to stop and smell the roses, as well as to sniff the grass to see whether any other dog had said hello lately. Hopefully, she gave thanks for an incredible sense of smell that was far beyond what we humans possess.

Peaches uses her sense of smell to check for any whiff of another dog.

18

·· ● ··

Manners Galore

Peaches was the quietest of any dog I've been around. When she barked, she always had a purpose in mind. Her intentions included,

"Watch me eat because I don't like to eat alone."

"Time for a walk."

"At least Glenda could share her donut with me."

"The doorbell is ringing."

"I'm at the back door and want to come out with you."

"Let me out so I can take care of business."

Peaches didn't bark without a good reason.

Some dogs didn't need an excuse to bark. In her younger days, Peaches barked at other dogs often. As she aged, the older, wiser version kept her barking to a minimum. The skill of listening rated much higher than the worthless habit of making noise. Peaches showed her manners in this way. May God forgive me for thinking it was more important to be heard than to listen to another soul.

When no one else was at the church, when it would be only Peaches and me, she was invited to go with me. Someone usually showed up to surprise us. After all, it was a pretty large, busy church. But Peaches was always excited when I asked her whether she wanted to go to church with me—outside of office hours, of course.

She loved going to the church, so I called her the "Church Dog." Once we were inside, Peaches would quietly sneak off from me so she could explore all the rooms, nooks, and crannies of the church. In a huge church, she wasn't easy to find. I had things to do and wasn't patient enough to spend my time looking for a dog. Again, she wasn't making any noise the way some dogs would. She enjoyed keeping away from me so she could give herself a minitour. After she got her exploring done, she usually came back to me. On rare occasions, after waiting for an extended time, I searched for her. And always found her.

We usually haven't thought of dogs as being polite. But she was. She was quick to get out of the way when she realized that Glenda or I was headed her way. It amazed me how Peaches was always happy to step aside for anyone walking her way. She moved over when meeting anyone on the sidewalk. When our grandson Bentley was playing baseball indoors and running in circles, she hurried to avoid getting run over. Perhaps it was survival of the fittest.

Whenever Peaches was lying on my lap and I told her that I needed to get up, she moved immediately. When Glenda and I were leaving the house, we moved her bed to the utility room. She saw it was moved and hopped right in. We didn't have to move her or ask her to jump in.

When I turned the television off, she heard the squiggly noise it made and automatically got down off my lap, even when I was staying in the recliner for a nap. When I got up in the middle of the night and she was sleeping beside me, she moved over so she was not in my way. Peaches was always polite about moving aside for someone else.

When she was around Scooter, Rachel's Yorkshire terrier, or Belle, Andrea's Yorkie, she accepted food given to her but never took food away from them. She took her food and didn't compete with the other dogs. I actually fed Peaches and Scooter in the same room, and no fight over food ever took place.

Peaches was not as prissy as I expected a half poodle to be. For the most part, she was outgoing, but she had brief spells when she needed time alone, content to lie in her basket. She slowly approached a stranger, cautiously gauging whether this person registered as friend or foe. She was loving to whoever she met on our walks. Yet she sometimes sensed trouble and backed off.

She greeted family members when we showed up at their house or they visited us. She implied, "Glad to see you," circling around them and barking. The family member understood her hint and picked her up to hold her. She gave our newborn granddaughter Hartley kisses.

Peaches was always glad to see Glenda and me when we have been gone. She showed the same joy for us, running in circles and barking. We too picked her up to hold her.

She made sure she was touching me when she slept. She always positioned herself on the left arm of the recliner and placed her side against the outside of my calf.

When we went for a walk, we sometimes encountered sprinklers watering the yard and sidewalk. She followed me into the street so we avoided getting soaked. She usually didn't slow me down too much when we were walking, although she had her days when she wanted to stay longer and roam around the grass. Especially on days when the weather was gorgeous.

You can easily see that Glenda and I have spent lots of time and effort to teach Peaches her manners. What an amazing job we have done! Not really. It was more Peaches than us. She deserved the credit for being so polite.

Glenda's first dog was a rat terrier named Charm. Rat terriers were bred as hunting dogs but became prevalent on family farms during the 1920s and 1930s. The rat terrier was first registered as an official breed by the AKC on July 1, 2010.

The American Kennel Club defines their temperament as "friendly, inquisitive, and lovable." It adds this:

> An American original, with a breed name said to
> be coined by Teddy Roosevelt, the Rat Terrier is a
> compact, tough, smooth-coated exterminator dog.
> Rat Terriers come in two size varieties and are happy-go-lucky, playful, and portable companions.
>
> Balanced, compactly built Rat Terriers are tough
> but elegant-looking. There are two size divisions:
> miniatures stand ten to thirteen inches; standards
> are over thirteen inches and as high as eighteen
> inches. The smooth, shiny coat comes in varieties
> of pied patterns (pied, a word borrowed from the
> horseman's lexicon, means 'comparatively large
> patches of one or more colors in combination with
> white'). These smoothly muscled exterminators are
> constructed for the efficient movement required for
> a long day's work.

Glenda remembered two dogs from her childhood that she thought were polite. She loved to recall her first dog, cherishing her memories of the black-and-white rat terrier named Charm. At the age of four, Glenda wandered off on the family farm with Charm. The dog stayed right beside her while Glenda fell asleep. Her family began looking for her, fearing that she was in the water tank or creek.

She was no easy find, so neighbors were called in to search for her. Charm stayed right with her. Eventually, a family member discovered Glenda sleeping, Charm by her side. The lost was finally found.

The other time—vivid in Glenda's memory—happened when she was about seven. Glenda played with Charm, dressing her up with a scarf around her neck. Underneath the scarf she had tied a rope, and she had tethered it to the screen door on the back porch. Glenda went inside to get a drink of water. When she got back, Charm was gone, and so was the rope.

The family spread out and scoured the farm. No luck. Glenda prayed, "Charm, come home. You've got to come home."

Charm did not come home. Every day after Charm came up missing, Glenda prayed the same prayer. "Charm, come home. You've got to come home."

Glenda's mother remembered how her daughter prayed the same prayer every day and every night. A week later, no Charm.

Glenda continued to pray for Charm every day with great feeling. "Charm, come home. You've got to come home."

Glenda didn't give up. With persistence, faith, and hope, she kept praying into the second week.

Finally, after two weeks in the wild, Charm came dragging home and scratched on the back screen. The rope was broken, mud covered her coat, and she was famished and bone-dry thirsty. But Glenda was tickled that her prayers were answered. Ah, Charm was finally home! Charm got a feast of chicken that evening to celebrate his return.

The other dog Glenda remembers was a yellow-colored greyhound named Buck. Glenda's father, Charles, raised many greyhounds, loving to race them and hunt coyotes with them. That worked
well because Buck loved to hunt coyotes and to race. In the greyhound
races, Buck always won. Glenda's dad was offered a lot of money for
Buck at different times, but he turned it down every time.

As with all good dogs, age finally hit Buck. He got old and couldn't
run any more. He was forced to retire from racing.

But he still wanted to hunt coyotes. Whenever Glenda's father
would leave the door open on the back of the coyote-hunting truck,
Buck seized the opportunity and jumped in. Out of habit, Charles
closed the rear door on his truck one day, unaware that Buck was
inside.

He looked for Buck for two days. Finally, it dawned on him to look
in the cage in the back of the truck. There was Buck, so happy to see
Charles. Would you be happy to see the guy who locked you up for
two days? Duh. I wouldn't. If a human had been caged up for two
days, it's a lock that that person would not be thrilled to see the rescuer.

Peaches was always glad to see me, even if I'd only been to work
for one day.

Buck continued to age; he couldn't even walk any more. The day
came when Charles knew he had to put Buck down, but he could
not do it. He put it off for lots of weeks, even months. After Charles
found the courage to commit the dastardly deed, he said it was the
longest day of his life.

"I just want to do what makes you happy," Buck, Charm, Peaches,
and many other dogs would simply say.

And that's the story of three dogs who were able to show their manners. Those three dogs can teach us a lesson. People of mercy, everyone who is for justice, remember how polite those three dogs were. See if you can match them with your manners. We can keep cool and show we too can treat others with manners galore.

*Peaches shows her manners by moving
to the edge of the sidewalk for a pedestrian.*

19

•• • ••

Who Gives the Dog a Bath?

Glenda has dealt with some serious allergies and asthma, often struggling to get her next breath. Three times, she wasn't sure the next breath would ever show up. She has stayed up in the middle of the night, praying the Lord's prayer, quoting the Twenty-Third Psalm, hoping the next breath would somehow arrive. She was on the verge of heaven, scared but holding on to hope that she might capture the all-important next breath.

We were advised by her allergy and asthma specialist to check in to National Jewish Health in Denver. Dr. Strickland had served his internship at National Jewish, and he has effectively added seventeen years to Glenda's life. We took three trips to the NJH facility that has earned a reputation for the best care in the world for respiratory issues.

Our insurance provider gave us two choices of doctors who were included in their network. We discovered one had a long foreign name. It wasn't for a lack of trusting him, but we weren't sure we would be able to understand his English. We chose the other option, Dr. Weber, who Dr. Strickland later told us is the best doctor in the world to diagnose and cure anyone with breathing problems. We were overwhelmed and thankful for that unexpected good news.

The first time we went there, tests were run on Glenda for nine days. She got tired of being poked and prodded. The results? Her bronchial tubes are "nearly to completely collapsed." Translation: she has very little space for the oxygen to pass through her bronchial tubes. And she is allergic to dogs, cats, mold, and mildew. Cats are her most serious allergy. When Glenda goes to visit someone with a cat, within five minutes she is turning red and sneezing. Consequently, we have never had a cat.

After Chihuahuas and shelties in the past—dogs that shed in clumps—we were thankful that we now had a Maltipoo who was hypoallergenic. It is ironic that Glenda chose a Maltipoo because at the time she had no idea that this combination of breeds did not shed or produce destructive dander. We feel it's no coincidence. Glenda picked out Peaches because she was so cute. Glenda says she has more breathing and coughing problems around our daughters' two Yorkies, Scooter and Belle, than around Peaches. God works in mysterious, miraculous ways.

After test results were complete, Dr. Weber looked them over and consulted with us. "You're a mess," he said to Glenda. He didn't know it, but Dr. Strickland had used the exact same words.

Three other doctors consulted with us after the test results were complete. Dr. Li was privy to the test results on allergies. She had a way of getting right to the point.

"Who gives the dog a bath?" she asked.

"I do," Glenda answered.

Dr. Li stared directly at me. Then she pointed her index finger at me. I was hearing the roar of the train rumbling down the tracks.

"That's your job now," she commanded.

Peaches detested the bath. The minute she saw me with a couple of towels in hand and am headed for the bathtub, she started shaking like a twig on a gale-force windy day. I tried to soothe her with my words.

"You'll be so clean and pretty," I said.

In spite of her fear, she gave me a kiss on my hand. She still loved me. It was always a battle to pull the dried matting from the corners of her eyes. That task was much easier if she was wet. She fought it.

"Don't you dare touch my eyes, my ears, my paws," was Peaches' message, backed up by a glare well punctuated by her body language and bark.

Our dog wanted to go outside to shake the water off once we were finished with the bath. She had a look of steel in her eyes. She was really mad at us for some time. Then she wanted to go under a towel and blanket in her bed.

"You look so clean and pretty," Glenda encouraged.

It took a while, but she got over her anger. At least she shut down any hint of a grudge quickly. A lesson well learned.

Peaches also hated going to the groomer. We tried all the options. After we took her to a nationally franchised pet store, the groomer said Peaches had demolished her thumbnail. I checked all her fingernails. None were missing or black and blue. Maybe the swelling hadn't arrived yet.

We took her to a Hispanic groomer whose price was quite reasonable, and we liked her work. End of problem. Or so we thought. She was good to us, and she was well loved by the other customers too. She was so popular that we soon had a problem trying to find an opening on her schedule. We knew when Peaches was shaggy and needed her fur trimmed; we couldn't wait months for it.

Next, we took Peaches to the nationally franchised pet store closer to our home. We came back to pick her up and were informed the groomer could not trim her ears and face because she wouldn't let him.

"Why pay all this money if they aren't going to do the job?" I asked, after leaving the pet shop.

I figured Glenda and I could do better and bought some clippers. We tried to groom her twice. There was cream-colored fur all over the kitchen. She snapped at us. She would not hold still. We found out it wasn't so easy to groom her, and those clippers have gathered dust in the garage ever since.

I looked through the dog groomers on my phone. There was one more groomer on our side of Wichita. We took Peaches there. The service was not adequate, and Peaches got a military haircut. The people who waited on me fell short of making me feel comfortable about leaving Peaches there.

A groomer in Wichita was now out of the question, so I looked for a plan B. Or C through Z. I decided to drive back to the groomer we had in our previous location in Marion. Even though it was a seventy-mile drive, it was worth it. Autumn took extra time explaining to us how she would clip Peaches. During hot summer weather, she always asked whether we wanted her fur cut shorter for the season.

Autumn at the grooming shop Critter Connection is a gifted groomer with an overwhelming love for animals—especially dogs and horses. She too was well aware that Peaches can be a challenge to groom. Autumn loved Peaches and was always kind, even when Peaches put her through a small-scale war zone.

On a Wednesday, Peaches and I journeyed the seventy miles to keep our appointment for Autumn to groom her. A colorful banner outside Critter Connection greets us. "Dogs Spoiled Here," it proclaimed. I find that slogan was truthful amid Autumn's willingness to share her gift. She was honest and made time to visit with us.

Autumn has been forced to use a small muzzle on Peaches at times, as well as a cloth sling with holes in it for the dog's legs when the groomer trims the legs and clips her paw nails. Peaches was unable to reach far enough to snap at her when the sling was in place. As Autumn said, "Peaches is not trying to bite me, just give a warning."

"Yes, Autumn, we know Peaches has a short leash, er, limit. She lets you know when she has reached her limit," I answered.

When I came back to pick up Peaches, Autumn said, "I didn't have to use the muzzle today, and Peaches was good. She didn't snap at me one time. Peaches gave me a kiss when I was finished grooming her."

"Peaches will be one hundred years old in dog years in only twenty-six days," I informed Autumn.

"She is still pretty spry," she responded.

A very vulnerable time for Peaches unfolded after she had been groomed. She was making a transition from lots of fur to very little fur. She wasn't able to tell me she was freezing, but I saw her shivering. I made sure she had a blanket under her and another one over her. She has often gotten quite ill after a grooming.

Likewise, when we walked and she slowed down to a crawl, she couldn't tell me that she was tired and her legs were giving out. There are days when I had to carry her home toward the end of our walk. I don't push her to go too fast, as I remember that Autumn told me she has a hip out of alignment.

The creation story also reminds us of our responsibility to take care of our animals. It's painful to see the news on TV of how shabby some animal owners can be—to see pictures of dogs or horses with their ribs sticking out and starving. It hurts to see that some owners haven't taken care of God's creatures.

Constant training that requires any owner's time is a vital part of the picture when we invite a pet into our family. It would be wise to set aside the time necessary to give the dog good training; no shortcuts or CliffsNotes will work.

The Maltese side of Peaches caused her to appear feisty in other situations. Glenda pulled the dried matting from her eyes between baths. Peaches got jumpy and unleashed a warning snap at her. This was not the "I'm trying to bite you" nip yet. Peaches employed that one only as a last resort. She had a few messages to warn us about her boundaries.

"Don't ever try to detach the dried matting from my eyes."

"Don't touch me while I'm eating."

"Never touch my paws or ears."

"Please don't carry me from my warm bed and blanket to the cold outdoors."

With her female intuition, Peaches sensed when Glenda was going to remove the matting from her eyes. She avoided Glenda and looked for a place to hide under the bed. If she won the race to under the bed, it was a major obstacle to remove her.

Peaches' coat grew really fast. The fur was soon down over her eyes before we got her back to the groomer. Glenda sometimes trimmed around her eyes. Again, Peaches figured out when that was coming. Glenda said, "Grab her, Dad."

In the last chapter, I praised Peaches for her manners. In this chapter, Peaches reminds us of the other side of her personality and the challenges she brings. She would have said, "Don't become too comfortable."

20

•• ● ••

The Spin Cycle

You thought a spin cycle is what happens when the washer spins the clothes at the end of a wash to drain any excess water away. You could have understood the spin cycle as what happens when a basketball player dribbles into the lane and performs an unbelievable spin to fool the defense and make a layup. But Peaches had a different perception of the spin cycle. It was what happens when she overflowed with excitement. Her spin cycle was when she turned circles around someone. It was her way of saying "Thank you."

Peaches never smiled. If her grade in school depended on a smile, she would have failed for sure. When Peaches felt as if she was walking on air, tickled pink, she went around and around in her spin cycle. We didn't have to wonder when she was happy. She also performed the spin cycle when she anticipated something good was about to happen.

It happened when she hadn't seen family in some time. When we went to see Andrea and Jeff in Omaha. When Kevin, Rachel, and Bentley came over. When Glenda came home after four days of work out of town. When I arrived home after working all day on Wednesday.

When she knew it was time for our daily walk, she twirled. She was in that spin cycle when we came home from a walk and she was pretty sure a treat was coming her way. Every time Peaches knew a treat was in store, she spun vigorously. She turned circles when I was in my recliner and slapped my thighs, the sign to jump up and lie in my lap.

"Come on, puppy. I want you with me," I said.

She appreciated my gesture. I placed a blanket over my legs. She loved to snuggle while resting between my knees.

The spin cycle for Peaches is like our Thanksgiving celebration. While my imagination blossoms in a monumental way, I ponder what she would have said about how Thanksgiving relates to her spin cycle.

Peaches could say, "Well, I am not able to talk, even though Balaam's ass did (Num. 22:28–30). But I am thankful I am able to communicate what I want to say in other ways (looks, nips, barks, growls, kisses).

"My spin cycle is how I celebrate Thanksgiving—not only on one day a year but every day of the year.

"I am so thankful for my family. For Momma, especially when she gives me a tiny bite of donut or ice cream. For Momma's shoulders because that's where I ride when we take a trip.

"For Daddy, even though he gives me oatmeal. For the tiny bites of fried yellow squash he gives me. For Daddy's lap because that's my favorite place to sleep.

"For Kevin, Rachel, and Bentley because they take good care of me when Momma and Daddy are out of town.

"For Andrea and Jeff because Andrea is the person who rescued me out of that cage when I was little. And they make sure I have plenty of food when I am at their house.

"For babies Hartley and Mia because they are so cute and sweet.

"For Scooter and Belle because sometimes we play together. I accept them as a part of my family too.

"For a warm house when I come in out of the cold. For a clean sweater when it's cold outside. For the dryer when hot clothes come out so I can jump on top and enjoy the warmth.

"For a shade tree or a pickup to lie under during the summer heat. Those are the days when this heavy coat of fur overheats me on my way to misery.

"For Christmas because I love ripping with my teeth into the stuffed animals and other toys I receive. For Christmas because I love bringing gifts the way the Wise Men did. A dead snake, a dead frog, a dead turtle, even if Momma didn't appreciate them. I don't understand why. For Christmas because of the animals beside the manger where the baby Jesus was born.

"For soft food and water. I love my soft food so much more than that old dry stuff they feed me. But one has to eat. I am so thankful for cold water after a walk during the heat of the summer.

"I am thankful for a walk on beautiful days but sad when it rains or snows because I can't breathe fresh air on those days. And it's too much when they expect me to hold it until the rain is over. That means I have to go out in the cold rain.

"For owners who show they trust me. I must have earned it because they give me a lot more freedom around here than they used to offer.

"For having no fear because I do not pace or bark when thunder booms. Even though strange noises startle me for a second, I am not afraid of them.

"For wisdom that grows as I age.

"There are so many more blessings God has given me. It's hard to fathom them all. I am even grateful for the spin cycle. It's my way of saying 'Yay! Hallelujah! Praise the Lord!'

"I see lots of people who could learn something from the spin cycle. They only talk negatively and fail to recognize the blessings when God pours them out. I hope they can learn to celebrate good news when it comes. I pray they learn the gift of gratitude."

As Peaches celebrated with her spin cycle, she demonstrated the fullness of joy in her heart, the outward sign of the complete joy she felt inside. Jesus said, "I have told you this so that my joy may be in you and that your joy may be complete" (John 15:11).

21

••●••

Yorkies: Belle and Scooter

Both of our daughters have Yorkies, officially known as Yorkshire terriers. Scooter and Belle are spunky, assertive, affectionate. They love to play, and they make good lapdogs. Yorkies are hypoallergenic because they have thick hair that resembles a human's hair much more than a dog's fur. They were first bred to chase the rats off in England during the nineteenth century.

The American Kennel Club says, "Beneath the dainty, glossy, floor-length coat of a Yorkshire Terrier beats the heart of a feisty, old-time terrier. Yorkies earned their living as ratters in mines and mills long before they became the beribboned lapdogs of Victorian ladies."

Yorkies are the tenth-most-popular dog breed and the most popular dog for city dwellers. Like Chihuahuas, they are small, never more than seven pounds, but still make protective watchdogs. Their small size and fierce, watchdog frame of mind create a good fit for living in the city. They overflow with personality. The AKC says they provide "years of laughs, love, and constant companionship."

Jeff and Andrea's Yorkie, Belle, is very affectionate. She loves to cuddle and have her tummy scratched. She gives kisses, unaffected by how many, until you have to move your hand away. She is always glad to see us when we visit Andrea and Jeff in Omaha. Belle is dark brown with a smidgen of black trim around her face, weighing in at just under five pounds. She is little lover; she loves to be hugged.

Belle shocked me one day after I had ridden many miles on a bicycle in Omaha. I love a bicycle trail in Omaha that starts in tiny Keystone Park near Fort and Ninetieth Streets. It meanders along a creek with no stops because the trail goes under every street, resulting in no worries about other traffic. The trail goes by Nebraska Furniture Mart, Aksarben (Nebraska spelled backward) with its shops and industry, and all the way to Plattsmouth and the Omaha municipal water plant. I had ridden a thirty-five-mile round trip on this perfect trail, enjoying the beautiful day.

I'll never forget that day because of the shock I received upon arrival at Andrea and Jeff's house. What caught my eye was that as I rode into their driveway on my Trek bike, both of them were sitting in their car. I knew both had gone to work earlier that morning. Both of them were crying. Their veterinarian had told them that Belle was terminal with a stomach disease. He said Belle had two months to live.

What a shock! That vet wanted to put Belle down, saying any other procedures or tests were useless. He diagnosed liver failure. He said it wouldn't help to test her blood. They asked whether there were any other options. The vet answered no and said Belle wasn't far away from heart failure.

"Is there any treatment you could do?" Glenda asked.

"No," he answered.

His fees for seeing Belle were the same as they paid for an overnight stay at the next stop. He had a big sign up in the office asking his customers to vote for him as the best vet in Omaha. Our family said no thanks.

They got a second opinion, driving to Kansas State University, where a team of vets gave a diagnosis that was night-and-day different from the first vet's opinion. Much more positive, the team worked with Belle, changed her diet, and told Andrea and Jeff she could never eat table food. She would have to be on a very strict diet for the rest of her life. These vets did their best to control her health.

The pleasant turn of events is that Belle has now lived six years past the original vet's diagnosis. She is healthy except for following the special diet. She is as loving as she ever was. Another wonderful turn of events is the kind vet who now gives Belle beyond-the-charts total care. Dr. Kate Vanden Hull has been so kind to Belle and the family, sometimes "forgetting" to charge them for appointments and other perks.

Belle has always had a voracious appetite, even before the vet ordered the special diet. Before the scary episode, Jeff once came home from work to find Belle lapping up huge bowls of water. She was parched-dry thirsty and just kept drinking water as they kept filling the bowl. Jeff wondered why. Later, he discovered some peppered beef jerky missing from his suitcase. Belle had gotten into it and evidently thought she had hit the jackpot.

Another time she got into the egg salad. A member of Jeff's family had hidden half an egg salad sandwich in his coat pocket. Belle found it. Belle devoured it. She kept it down.

Jeff and Andrea have been really careful about keeping Belle out of human food that would be hard on her stomach and would trigger her permanent disease. But one Thanksgiving, she found an abandoned plate and added shrimp tail to her diet. Thankfully, it did not stay down. When Belle goes sniffing for food, no one can leave any food plates too low or unguarded.

Belle wastes no time snarfing food down. Each day, she eats one-fourth of a cup of dry digestive care food during four feedings and a small helping of moist food that smells like slop. Each time she eats, the food's gone in half a minute. She also takes a tiny dose of prednisone each day.

A Yorkie who became famous during World War II and deserves our recognition was named Smoky. The four-pound dog was found in an abandoned foxhole in the New Guinea jungle. American soldiers thought she belonged to the Japanese but soon discovered she didn't understand their language. Corporal William Wynne took the dog under his wing, sleeping with Smoky in his tent and feeding her Spam and C rations.

Smoky protected 250 men from the bombs of enemy attacks by navigating through an eight-inch pipe for seventy feet to deliver a telegraph wire in the dark, even though half the pipe was blocked by dirt and mud. Smoky parachuted out of a tree from thirty feet above ground. Never ill, she survived heat, humidity, flying on 150 air raids on New Guinea, and a typhoon hitting Okinawa. Corporal Wynne credited her with saving his life multiple times.

Smoky learned many tricks, entertaining the troops in New Guinea, Australia, Korea, and in between. After the war, Smoky and Wynne traveled to Hollywood and around the world, demonstrating her tricks, which included walking a tightrope while blindfolded. Smoky performed on forty-two live television shows without ever repeating a trick.

Also known as "Yorkie Doodle Dandy," the dog was credited with being the first therapy dog, as she accompanied nurses to the military hospitals. The commanding officer was the famous Dr. Charles Mayo, who allowed Smoky to go on hospital rounds. Smoky earned eight battle stars and accompanied twelve combat missions. She lived to the age of fourteen and is buried in the Cleveland Metroparks' Rocky River Reservation in Lakewood, Ohio. On Veterans Day 2005, a sculpture of Smoky by Susan Bahary was unveiled above his burial plot.

While not as famous, Rachel and Kevin's Yorkie, Scooter, has made some rescues of his own. He is affectionate and keeps licking for a long time like Belle. This little Yorkie is skinny with more black than brown fur—as his entire face is a light tan. Scooter weighs in at five pounds, lives in constant motion, can never sit still except when Kevin gives him a haircut or he's lying on a lap. He is high energy, always on the move. Scooter has the longest tongue, so when you least expect it, he will give you a kiss—clear up into your nostrils. Yuck!

This skinny Yorkie likes to sleep on Kevin's lap—or Glenda's lap when we keep him. He runs with the speed of a cheetah. Having chased him for blocks, I can attest to his running skill. Kevin has repeatedly run after him in their neighborhood. We have to make sure he is on a leash outdoors because he likes to run away. In a split second, he's gone. Being so light, he can also jump high. Jumping up onto the couch or a high bed is a breeze for Scooter.

Scooter barks when he sees another dog on television. Scooter is amazing because he never misses a dog or other animal on the TV screen. Glenda and I have made the mistake of falling asleep with the TV still blasting while Scooter was staying with us. A dog appeared on the screen, and Scooter woke us up with a jolting bark. The only way to quiet him down was to say, "You got that dog, Scooter."

He is also quick to bark when he spies a dog next door from his watchtower on the top of the couch. He barks whenever the dogs next door come out to play.

Scooter has earned his keep by protecting Bentley. Rachel was in the shower when Bentley was six months old. Scooter came to the bathroom and scratched rapidly at the door. Rachel knew that when Scooter barked, it usually wasn't any kind of emergency. She also knew that when he scratched, it meant something significant. Once Rachel quickly scurried to Bentley's room, she found him hanging by his feet over the rail of his bassinet. If not for Scooter's scratching on the shower door, Bentley likely would have fallen over the edge of the bassinet onto the floor.

A second time, their Yorkie came scratching at Rachel's leg when Bentley was only one year old. Rachel hurried to find Bentley. She found Bentley at the top of the staircase, ready to head down seventeen steps. Scooter had saved Bentley twice. The five-pound watchdog remained on guard for Bentley's safety at all times.

Likewise, two other dogs named Bella and Sadie made their own miraculous rescue. The headline from Eric Alvarez at First Coast News, Channel 2, of Jacksonville, Florida, shouted from the rooftops: "Loyal dogs rescue owner after stroke."[1] Their owner, Maureen Hatcher of St. Augustine, suffered a stroke in her home on December 3, 2018. The last thing she remembered was taking a shower.

"I remember Sadie coming in," Hatcher said. "I said, 'Mommy needs help,' and then they were gone."[2]

It was fortunate that a neighbor saw the two Labrador retrievers running loose on the street—she knocked on Hatcher's door.[3]

Hatcher said she wasn't sure how the dogs got out because the door locks automatically. She thinks the door must have been left slightly ajar.

The neighbor knocked on Hatcher's door, and after receiving no answer, she came inside to find her. She then called 911.

Instead of taking Hatcher to the closest emergency room, paramedics took her to the comprehensive stroke center at Baptist Medical Center in Jacksonville. Dr. Nima Aghaebrahim said that particular decision probably prevented permanent brain damage. "When a stroke happens, time is everything," Aghaebrahim said.

Doctors used a medical procedure that wasn't discovered until recently to remove the blood clot.

"By rights, I shouldn't be in the shape I'm in," Hatcher said with Bella and Sadie at her feet. "I am blessed...very blessed."

Everything worked together in this story to make it far from coincidental. A door was ajar; her dogs looked for help; a neighbor showed up; Hatcher was taken to a stroke specialty unit; a new medical procedure was used. It all began with the quick thinking of Sadie and Bella, the two dogs who saved Hatcher.

Consider a time a dog saved Glenda, who was living in a duplex, sharing an apartment with someone she seldom saw. They both worked as nurses, Glenda on the day shift and Carol on the night shift.

Once in the middle of the night, when Carol was working and Glenda was home alone, Gretchen, Glenda's Chihuahua, awakened her with some loud barking. It was a drenching, hot summer night, and Glenda had left the window open. She looked out her bedroom window and saw a man in a white T-shirt smoking a cigarette. Glenda screamed and called the police—afraid, but grateful Gretchen had awakened her.

Glenda remembered that the same man drove down the alley behind her apartment every morning. She thought he was a Peeping Tom. It didn't help matters that a serial killer who had done some of his damage in her neighborhood was featured in the local news headlines. Thankfully, Glenda knew he had already been incarcerated. Still, those memories of the murderer in the news added to her fear.

Five dogs saved someone in this chapter. Smoky, Scooter, Bella, Sadie, and Gretchen were alert and ready to spring into action. Since the term "rescue dog" applies to a different kind of dog, call them emergency dogs. They all rose to the occasion when an individual was in an emergency.

Scooter, Peaches, and Belle relax with Dan.

22

•• ● ••

Lassie and Rin Tin Tin

Six o'clock on Sunday evening. As a child, I looked forward to watching *Lassie* at that precise hour each week. Whatever drama dictated the plot, Lassie kept cool and calm. She helped rescue people in danger. Lassie was my first dog heroine, a canine who could handle any crisis. Of course, it was the background music that warned us viewers when trouble was imminent and when victory was about to win the day.

The show *Lassie* lasted nineteen years, from 1954 through 1973. A new series began in the eighties, and an animated one titled *The New Adventures of Lassie* ran from 1997 through 1999.[1]

Lassie was a heroine to lots of successive generations. The theme of *Lassie* was first given life over 160 years ago by a short story written by Elizabeth Gaskell in 1859 called "The Half-Brothers." The story's heroine is a collie named Lassie. I'll summarize its content: two half brothers are dying in the snow, and Lassie leads a search party to them. One half brother survives. One does not.

Lassie was also shaped by a true story that took place during World War I. Unfortunately, five hundred English sailors died when a German submarine torpedoed a Royal Navy battleship. A local pub at Lyme Regis volunteered its cement basement to serve as an improvised mortuary. Lassie, a mixed-breed collie, went to the basement and kissed one of the sailors. She also lay beside that same sailor, warming him up, and he eventually survived. From that time on, sailors loved to tell the story of how Able Seaman John Cowan was miraculously saved by the dog Lassie.

Later on, Lassie appeared as a fictional character created by Eric Knight. He wrote a short story about a collie; that story appeared in the *Saturday Evening Post* in 1938. It later morphed into a novel called *Lassie Come Home* in 1940.

From 1943 through 1951, seven movies about Lassie premiered in theaters across America. Lassie was first played by Pal, a rough collie, who was trained by Rudd Weatherwax. Pal's descendants later played Lassie. The 1943 movie *Lassie Come Home* starred Elizabeth Taylor and Roddy McDowall. In 1945, *Son of Lassie* came out, starring Peter Lawford and June Lockhart.

In my childhood naivete, I was sure all Lassie's heroic rescues were the gospel truth in every scene. How could anyone possibly call them fiction? They sure seemed real, anyway. Yet behind the movie scenes were writers and producers who were dreaming up each story line.

Now that I am older, it only makes sense that *Lassie* was never intended to be believed as the literal facts. The episode "The Runaway" airs about halfway through the fourth season. A young couple (Cloris Leachman as Ruth Martin, Jon Shepodd as Paul Martin) have bought the farm and discover in their barn a seven-year-old runaway named Timmy, played by Jon Provost. How many seven-year-olds have you known who have run away from home with no thought of wanting to go back home?

In a 1964 episode, when nearly the entire cast had been replaced, the Martins have decided to leave the farm and venture to Australia so Paul can teach farmers down under how to grow crops. From then on, the show focuses on Lassie spending time with forest laborers. How many farmers have you known who left the farm and went to Australia?

In 2004, June Lockhart described *Lassie* as a "fairy tale about people on a farm in which the dog solves all the problems in twenty-two minutes, in time for the last commercial." This is the same Lockhart who, along with Jan Clayton, were the only members of the show to win an Emmy for her acting. Jon Provost later received a star on the Hollywood Walk of Fame.

More fantasy than fact, Lassie was the queen of the miracle rescuers. Yet she was what people wanted to see on black-and-white TV during the fifties and sixties. From 1957 through 1964, *Lassie* ranked in the top twenty-five in Nielsen ratings every year except 1960, when it was competing in prime time with *Walt Disney Presents* on ABC and *Shirley Temple Theater* on NBC. *Lassie* ranked thirteenth in 1963 and fifteenth in 1959 and 1961. It also ranks as the fifth-longest-running scripted prime-time show, lasting nineteen years on television.

Similar miraculous adventures actually appear in today's newspapers, online stories, and movies. Not all of them are fiction. Dogs named Odin, Frida, Bella, Sadie, and Smoky have actually saved others with their quick thinking. In one episode after the Martin family left for Australia, Lassie rescued a fox in the wild. No doubt, Odin would have done the same. Those are just the famous dogs who made the headlines. Many others who did not make the news rescued someone in an emergency.

The stories of Lassie remind us of a dog's intelligence and compassion in the face of danger. Lassie loves Timmy and protects him.

These stories remind me that in spite of the drama and trauma dogs have brought to my life, they have also kindly given love and compassion. It's time we give these dogs a little more credit. Thanks to Timmy and Lassie for this positive reminder.

The story of Rin Tin Tin also goes back quite a while in time. It began over a century ago, as the first Rin Tin Tin was born September 10, 1918, in Lorraine, France.[2] Rin Tin Tin was an early rescue dog. A German shepherd, he was rescued from a World War I battlefield by an American soldier named Lee Duncan, who had spent his boyhood in an orphanage. Duncan found Rin Tin Tin in a bombed dog kennel in France. Rin Tin Tin was trained by Duncan, who gave him the nickname Rinty.

Rin Tin Tin was from the same era as another German shepherd named Strongheart, who was born in Poland. Strongheart appeared in silent movies until he died in 1929. Like Rin Tin Tin, he appeared in national magazines and newspapers, as well as being proclaimed a star on the radio.

Strongheart still today has his picture on dog food cans. Both Strongheart and Rin Tin Tin impacted that generation with their likenesses on cereal boxes, on shoe polish cans, as Cracker Jack prizes, as figurines, and in children's books. They both influenced the public to invite German shepherds into their homes as family pets.

The trained dog Rin Tin Tin appeared in twenty-seven silent films—including *Frozen River* in 1929. He also appeared in four sound movies. As Rin Tin Tin was receiving twelve thousand fan letters each week, he was known as "the dog who saved Hollywood" because his movies kept Warner Brothers from going bankrupt.

Susan Orlean, in her book *Rin Tin Tin: The Life and the Legend*, says that the German shepherd won the vote for best actor in 1929.[3] This embarrassed the people in charge, and they changed the rules so that no animal could be nominated. The award then went to Emil Jennings.

Rin Tin Tin died August 10, 1932, causing a national emergency and resulting in deep mourning. Radio programs were cut in on so news of his death could be broadcast over the air waves. An hour-long broadcast about Rin Tin Tin aired the next day. He was buried in Asnières-sur-Seine, a famous pet cemetery near Paris, after he was returned to his country of birth.

Many generations of descendants also attained celebrity status, extending the Rin Tin Tin name for many years. He had a puppy in the next generation, Rin Tin Tin Jr. Then, Rin Tin Tin III helped promote military jobs for dogs in World War II. Lee Duncan again trained Rin Tin Tin IV for his acting career in the popular series in the fifties, but the German shepherd did not play the part well, so Flame Jr. ended up as the lead dog. Today, Rin Tin Tin XII is owned by Dorothy Yanchak, and that dog shows up for public events and keeps the influence of the family heritage flourishing.[2]

Lassie and Rin Tin Tin provided a heroine and hero for a TV-viewing generation of the fifties and later decades. They gave us an adventure in every show. They showed us courage, intelligence, and love in each episode. With their communicative eyes, TV stars Lassie and Rin Tin Tin spoke to us, sparking emotions from love to grief. With apologies to today's younger crowd who didn't see them each week, I can say that these dogs inspired a love for dogs among young viewers during those years when Lassie and Rin Tin Tin were starring on the television screen. Only three animals have ever been awarded stars on the Hollywood Walk of Fame. Their names? Lassie, Rin Tin Tin, and Strongheart.

23

•• ● ••

Bentley's Challenge

The very nature of the poodle breed is its difficulty in getting along with small children. Bruce Fogle writes, "Miniature and Toy Poodles tend to be picky and excitable and therefore are not suited to be around small children."[1] Add in the fact that poodles are pretty sensitive. Going back for centuries, since poodles were first bred over a thousand years ago, it was inherent that small children were never their favorite people.

The above quote requires that we define the three different sizes of poodles. A standard poodle is one that is over fifteen inches tall. Miniature poodles range in height from ten inches to fifteen inches. And a toy poodle is less than ten inches tall. Peaches falls into the category of the toy poodle.

Peaches was almost eleven, seventy-six in dog years, when Bentley was born. That was a great day for Bentley's grandparents and parents, but Peaches wasn't quite ready to agree. We offered Bentley our love, but Peaches wasn't yet willing to do the same. Just like the poodle, the Maltese breed has not done well in getting along with small children. Both Bentley and Peaches competed for my attention. They showed jealousy only when one thought the other was receiving more attention.

When Bentley was a year old, he tried to make friends with Peaches. But he didn't understand how to do that yet, sometimes pulling her hair. Peaches would snap at him. She hit her target a few times—too often—but as far as I know, she never broke the skin.

They withdrew from each other, doing their best to tolerate the other. Peaches tried to stay out of Bentley's way. Bentley played his football, baseball, basketball, boxing, and wrestling while ignoring Peaches. All the while, our family was doing our best to foster a friendship between the two.

Bentley felt immensely frustrated and repeatedly said, "Peaches doesn't like me."

Peaches chose to rest on the recliner, distant from danger, when Bentley was coming to our house. If she thought Bentley was playing too rowdily, she would mope along to another room.

Eventually, as Bentley neared three years old, he understood the need to pet Peaches softly. Peaches responded by licking Bentley's hand, giving him a kiss.

Still, the competition for Grandpa's attention didn't end. Peaches would be lying between my knees while I was flat on my back on the floor. Bentley decided it was time to wrestle or play football. He told Peaches to move. She moved, but she wasn't happy about it, slowly walking away with her head down.

Gradually, both of them began accepting the other competitor as part of the family. Then Glenda and I drove to Colorado for a wedding, leaving Peaches with Kevin and Rachel. One evening, both Kevin and Rachel tried to feed Peaches by hand. She wouldn't eat.

The next morning, Kevin and Rachel asked Bentley whether he would try to feed Peaches. He responded with a yes and attempted his own effort to feed Peaches. She ate when Bentley handed her the hard dog food. She wolfed down only what Bentley fed her but not what either of his parents tried to feed her.

As Bentley grew older, their relationship continued to grow as a bond. Bentley knew enough not to pull Peaches' fur anymore. He didn't intentionally throw toys at her except occasionally when he hadn't had a nap. He even said, "I love you, Peaches."

How did Peaches respond? She was not afraid to sit on the couch with Bentley anymore. Some days, she was eager to go with us to their house. Other days, the ninety-nine-year-old wanted to rest, so we let her stay home. She has also done her part to show acceptance of Bentley. She was not afraid of hanging out with the three-year-old. Their relationship to each other continued to grow.

Bentley included Peaches in his games. When Bentley needed another body for his baseball game, he told Peaches she could be the "oompire," as he pronounced it. In Bentley's judgment, Peaches just wasn't ready to be the pitcher, the catcher, or an outfielder. He said, "Peaches, you can be the 'oompire.'"

Sometimes Bentley allowed Peaches to come into his "locker room," and sometimes he didn't.

Peaches wanted to be included in Bentley's sports games. We tried to protect her, telling her to stay on the couch when the games got too rough. Peaches has been run over by a three-year-old, been hit by a flying plastic baseball and bat, and had to run for her life to avoid being hit. After all that, she didn't want to lie on the couch and watch; she wanted to stay in the middle of the action.

When Bentley's afternoon nap time rolled around, who slept together on Grandpa's lap? Bentley and Peaches.

We were at Kevin and Rachel's house one evening when Peaches wanted to go with us. After an hour, during which we all played baseball inside with a plastic ball, Peaches went to the front door and spent fifteen minutes there.

Bentley knew why. He asked, "Peaches, are you ready to go home?"

Bentley showed no fear in holding his hand out to Peaches, and at 101 years of age, she kissed his hand when he held it out to her.

Bentley loved all kinds of fruit. Strawberries, grapes, apples, and peaches. His mother said, "That was all I ate when I was pregnant with Bentley."

We told Bentley we would dish out some peaches for his dinner, and our puppy was sure we were talking about her. She knew that word. Peaches looked so proud, convinced that we were rattling on about her. She beamed, on fire in her own pride. Her chest swelled up, even jolting her head back.

In the real world, it's not always about us, even when we think it is. Of prime importance is to look at the big picture. How are my actions and words affecting others? The apostle Paul wrote, "Do nothing out of selfish ambition or vain conceit. Rather, in humility value others above yourselves, not looking to your own interests but each of you to the interests of the others" (Phil. 2:3–4).

Grandchildren Bentley and Hartley pet Peaches.

24

•••••

Kisses for Kids

"Today is a beautiful day in the neighborhood," sings Mr. Rogers. "It's a beautiful day in KAKEland," as the deejay Gene Rump used to say. It was an April day in the low eighties with gorgeous redbud trees in bloom, green grass in need of a lawn mower, and stunning flowers blooming. As Peaches and I walked past the children's playground just a block away from our house, eight children were enjoying the day on swings and slides while four parents supervised.

Peaches had walked only two houses away when two girls on bicycles stopped us to ask whether they could pet her. After Peaches sauntered past them, I picked her up and held her so a ten-year-old and a nine-year-old could pet her.

"She is so cute," the older one said.

"Thank you. Guess how old she is," I responded.

She gave me a blank look, as if she had no idea.

"Fourteen," I said.

No comment. The older girl noticed the pink sweater Peaches was wearing. "Isn't it too hot for a sweater?" she asked.

"You're right. It is."

I waited until we got a house away before taking the sweater off.

We had journeyed further on our walk when a boy about eight rolled by us on a scooter. Through the sound of metal wheels on a concrete sidewalk, he yelled, "I love your dog."

Peaches and I were about a block past him when a nine-year-old boy came up behind us on his bike. I scooted over, and Peaches followed so he could get by on the sidewalk. But he didn't go by. He stopped.

"I like your dog," he said.

"Thank you," I said. "It's a great day for a bike ride."

"It ain't mine." And off he rode.

For the most part, Peaches has been tolerant around children. She was much friendlier around teens and adults. She was not patient with toddlers who haven't learned to refrain from pulling her hair. She was willing to let older children pet her and even gave them a kiss on command.

Six-year-old twins, a girl and a boy, lived across the street from us. Berkley, the girl, loved Peaches. She got quite concerned, almost panicking, when Peaches walked near the street. She watched from her window with great fear. When I came out of the house alone, she always asked where Peaches was. She wanted to pet her. I reminded her that Peaches usually stayed out of the street.

The boy, Braxton, observed, watching Peaches while not showing quite as much affection toward her as Berkley. As we've watched these twins grow and become more mature, Peaches has grown in her relationship with them. She was not as defensive as she was when the twins were small.

The cutest little boy came by our house, asking to pet Peaches. Accompanied by his mother, he was five years old and always wore his fireman boots. He was bright and funny, and typical for that age, sometimes more honest than his mother wanted him to be. He was pretty sure that when he grows up, he will be hanging out at the fire station and fighting fires exactly like his dad. He wanted to pet Peaches, and she liked him.

Peaches and I made lots of friends with children who passed by on the sidewalk with their parents. I let them pet her and asked Peaches to give them a kiss.

During those times when Peaches and I were in a parking lot waiting for Glenda to finish shopping, we would see a small child with the parents. Every time Peaches wagged her tail. She wanted to make new friends. And we've made a lot of friends while in the car at a shopping mall.

"Awww, she gave me a kiss!" exclaimed a four-year-old little girl. She was excited, squealing with glee.

When we met children on our daily stroll, I always asked Peaches to give each one a kiss. But first I questioned the child about whether she wanted to pet the dog. Little two-year-old children were often afraid and said no. Or if the children did pet her, they were fearful and barely touched her. But the older ones were overjoyed to be offered the opportunity to pet her. Their parents were always happy about that too.

Marion Bond West shares a magical story about a child and a dog in *Daily Guideposts 2019*.[1] Marion and her husband, Gene, were squabbling near income tax time. Gene spread stacks of paper all over, including on the floor, while preparing taxes.

"I hate clutter!" Marion screamed.

"Don't lecture me!" Gene shouted.

They were arguing so loudly they almost didn't hear the doorbell ring.

It was six-year-old Mary Beth, who lived nearby.

"I'm selling these pictures I drew," said Mary Beth. "Someone we know in another state has a very sick dog, and my sister and I are sending a contribution."

Gene made room on the table, and Mary Beth spread out her bold, happy pictures.

"They are beautiful," said Marion, almost in tears.

Gene paid more than the dollar Mary Beth asked for each picture.

"Thank you both," said Mary Beth with an endless smile.

"Thank you, honey." Gene beamed, and Marion hugged her.

A little child came, bringing peace to the Bond household.

I love the way children respond in loving a pet. My nephew Tyler connected with the family dog at a very early age. In the presence of a babysitter, he addressed the family's Golden retriever. He said, "Look at the moon, Zach." His love for dogs continued to grow. Tyler met his future bride, Liz, at a dog park in Austin, Texas. Then Tyler and Liz included their dogs in their wedding; the dogs marched in and stood with the wedding party as groomsman and bridesmaid.

It simply makes my day when I see a child offering love to a dog. Innocence and compassion are always united in that beautiful picture.

The disciples of Jesus were trying their best to keep the children away from Him; the disciples were convinced it was their job to screen His calls. But Jesus wanted to relate to children.

Jesus said, "Let the little children come to me, and do not hinder them, for the kingdom of heaven belongs to such as these" (Matt. 19:14).

Jesus also said, "Unless you change and become like little children, you will never enter the kingdom of heaven" (Matt. 18:3).

25

·· ● ··

Francis of Assisi

Not only is Francis of Assisi the patron saint of Italy, but he is also remembered as the patron saint of animals. Catholic, Anglican, and some Protestant churches observe a blessing of the animals on the feast day of October fourth. That date commemorates the nearly eight-hundred-year anniversary of Francis's death on October 3, 1226.[1]

Saint Francis was also the one who started the custom of a live Christmas nativity scene in 1223. It unveiled to the audience's view a live ox and donkey on each side of the manger. There is a lot of sound biblical evidence to support Saint Francis's all-encompassing love for animals. Because his love was inclusive of all the animals, he would have loved Peaches, and she would have loved him.

After the great flood, God established a covenant with Noah and his sons that extends to all living creatures. Genesis 9:15–16 reads, "I will remember my covenant between me and all living creatures of every kind. Never again will the waters become a flood to destroy all life. Whenever the rainbow appears in the clouds, I will see it and remember the everlasting covenant between God and all living creatures of every kind on the earth." "All living creatures" is emphasized twice; not one living creature is left out of this covenant.

Saint Francis wrote a hymn titled "All Creatures of Our God and King," also known as "Canticle of the Creatures," or "Praises of Creatures." Written about 1225, although it refers to brother wind, mother earth, and sister moon, it surely includes the animals as creatures. The last verse proclaims, "Let all things their Creator bless, and worship him in humbleness, O praise Him! Alleluia!"

The scriptures often single out specific animals as being close to God's heart. One of those is the lamb. Isaiah 40:11 says, "He tends his flock like a shepherd; he gathers his lambs in his arms and carries them close to his heart; he gently leads those that have young." Wow! God carries the lamb close to His heart. What love! The Lamb of God, His Son, Jesus Christ, was also very close to His heart.

Another animal the Bible highlights is the bird. In Matthew 6:26 we read, "Look at the birds of the air; they do not sow or reap or gather into barns, and yet your heavenly Father feeds them." And Jesus said these words in Matthew 10:29: "Are not two sparrows sold for a penny? Yet not one of them will fall to the ground outside your Father's care." We are reminded of God's compassion bubbling over for even the sparrows.

Saint Francis must have taken these words to heart, for he preached to the birds. The following comes from the book *The Little Flowers of St. Francis.*

> He (Francis) said to his companions: 'Wait for me here on the road. I am going to preach to my sisters, the birds….The substance of St. Francis' sermon to those birds was this: 'My little bird sisters, you owe much to God, your Creator, and you must always and everywhere praise Him'….Thereby they

signaled that, just as St. Francis—who was to bear
the marks of Christ's Cross—had preached to them
and made the sign of the Cross over them, so they
had separated in the form of a cross and Flown
away, singing…[2]

Francis also helped tame a troublemaking wolf. In Gubbio where
Francis lived was

a large and fierce wolf which was so rabid with hunger it devoured not only animals but even human
beings. Francis had compassion on the townsfolk,
and so he went up into the hills to find the wolf.
Soon, fear of the animal had caused all of his companions to flee, though the saint pressed on. When
he found the wolf, he made the sign of the cross and
commanded the wolf to come to him and hurt no
one. Miraculously, the wolf closed his jaws and lay
down at Francis's feet.

'Brother Wolf, you do much harm in these parts and
you have done great harm in this region, and you
have committed horrible crimes by destroying God's
creatures without any mercy,' said Francis. 'All these
people accuse you and curse you…But brother wolf,
I would like to make peace between you and the
people.' Then Francis led the wolf into the town,
and surrounded by startled citizens made a pact
between them and the wolf. Because the wolf had
"done evil out of hunger," the townsfolk were to

feed the wolf regularly. In return, the wolf would no
longer prey upon them or their flocks. In this manner Gubbio was freed from the menace of the pred-
ator. Francis even made an agreement on behalf of
the town dogs, that they would not bother the wolf
again. Finally, to show the townspeople that they
would not be harmed, Francis blessed the wolf.[3]

Although some may wonder about the truth of this story, I have
no trouble believing it.

I went out to run in Douglass one Saturday morning, intent on
running a three-mile square on the outskirts of town. To my surprise,
I looked up to see a wolf; it proceeded to run with me. He seemed
peaceful, nothing close to violent. I felt no fear of him, and he seemed
pretty comfortable with me.

I can still hear the booming cadence of his huge paws as they
struck the pavement. It made noises louder than any animal (or human) I ever ran alongside. We ran together for a little over a mile, and
then he turned off and ran another direction. Someone had tamed
that wolf, although that person's training methods likely differed from
those of Francis of Assisi.

Psalm 145:21b reads, "Let every creature praise his holy name
for ever and ever."

In Psalm 148:7,10, we read, "Praise the Lord from the earth, you
great sea creatures and all ocean depths...wild animals and all cattle,
small creatures and flying birds..."

God included all his creatures in his covenant, his care and his
joy, knowing all of them are blessed with the ability to praise him.

26

•• • ••

A Scary Illness

Horrified. That's what I was feeling when Peaches suffered with a serious illness. How well I remember the signs when Lady Luck, our sheltie, was getting close to death. Her stomach was making loud, gurgling noises. She no longer wanted to be close to us. She would go to the front porch to be alone. She would go from the garage into the backyard to be alone. She was hurting.

Glenda was at least willing to take Lady to the veterinarian. Fearing the worst, I wasn't willing to go. The vet said her stomach was riddled with cancer. She said the best thing we could do was to put her out of her suffering.

Glenda was the one who had taken Lacey, our Chihuahua, to the vet to be put under, to be relieved of her pain. I had made a promise to Glenda that when Peaches came to that point of no return, it was my turn to take her to the vet. Peaches was now ninety-six in dog years. I was pretty sure she wasn't far from the end.

She had always been so well trained and didn't fail to bark to tell us to let her out to take care of business. She had gotten to the point that she barked at four in the morning when she had to go. Before that, she was usually able to hold it for six to eight hours before needing to mark.

Then one day, all that changed. She left lots of deposits all over the carpet in the master bedroom. The next day, we found multiple patches of diarrhea on the beige carpet outside the bathroom. I cleaned her messes up in both cases, and Glenda applied stain remover on the carpet and scrubbed it.

Peaches wouldn't eat. With her heavy coat, she usually didn't want a blanket on top of her but liked to lie over a blanket. Suddenly, she wanted us to cover her up. She was shaking more than Tina Turner, constantly unable to control her tremors from the cold. Glenda said we should take her to the vet, but I was afraid of what the vet would say and do. In simpler words, I was afraid the vet would want to put her down. As these symptoms lingered into the third day, I prayed for Peaches to get well.

We were used to her barking when Glenda and I ate. That still wasn't happening.

I checked the guide containing information about Maltipoos. It said the life expectancy of the Maltese breed is ten to thirteen years. Peaches was two months short of fourteen. These facts brought no consolation. I feared this was her goodbye.

Losing a dog, I remembered from some of the previous dogs we were forced to bury, can be almost as tough as watching one of our human loved ones cross the river. By now, I was fully aware of just how major a blow it would be to lose her.

On the fifth day, we were relieved as we watched her eat a little bit. On the sixth day, she began to act like herself. She even barked to go outside and for me to take her on a walk. I felt relieved to be able to grant her wish, and we walked. Later, she ate as if she were starved. Gradually, she transformed into the same dog we had known before her illness.

I didn't forget the fear I had known about losing Peaches, but I was so happy she was the real Peaches again! Thank you, God! You answer prayer.

Jesus said, "Until now you have not asked for anything in my name. Ask and you will receive, and your joy will be complete" (John 16:24). Yes, my joy was overwhelmingly complete.

Considering that Jesus was birthed by the Holy Spirit, James was his half brother. Joseph was the father of James but not the father of Jesus. The same James and the apostle Peter were the two primary leaders who spoke at a crucial Jerusalem Council in Acts 15:1–21. James also shares his wisdom about prayer. He writes, "And the prayer offered in faith will make the sick person well; the Lord will raise them up" (James 5:15).

Earlier in the same book of the Bible James wrote, he emphasizes the importance of believing when we pray. He says, "But when you ask, you must believe and not doubt, because the one who doubts is like a wave of the sea, blown and tossed by the wind. That person should not expect to receive anything from the Lord" (James 1:6–7).

I gradually changed my impression of Peaches to appreciate her so much differently than I did when we first got her. I learned to see her as a tough dog who did her best to fight through a serious illness. No longer did I see her as a prissy dog. The American Kennel Club agrees. It says, "There's the old stereotype of Poodles as foofy velvet pillow dogs looking down their long noses at us. Not true. Poodles are eager-to-please, highly trainable 'real dogs.' They like to work closely with their humans and can master all kinds of tricks and dog sports."

Modern Dog magazine points out some of their good qualities, especially their sense of humor. It says, "All Poodles are lively, fun-loving, affectionate, and intelligent, and many owners say the breed has a sense of humor to rival Seinfeld."

Now that our dog had shown loyalty, obedience, and unconditional love, we had the opportunity to show the same qualities to Peaches before she was gone, before we have lost that chance. I dreaded the day when the possibility to show that love to Peaches would be taken from me. Lesson for today: don't wait until they are gone from earth to show love. It works the same for dogs as it does for our human loved ones and friends.

Peaches, Glenda, and I felt a closer bond blossom between us because of this serious illness. Fortunately, Peaches was still licking with her kisses. She hasn't given up on life just yet.

27

•• ● ••

Aging Gracefully

A former teacher I respect, at ninety-seven years of age, still regularly rides her bicycle on fourteen-mile trips. I have played tennis with men in their nineties who were still skillful at handling a racquet. Fauja Singh, born in India, finished a 10K race at 101 years old. These are all people we can admire. These people have accomplished the art of aging gracefully in their physical health, a vision I want to hang on to when I reach their age. Similarly, it's a joy to learn from the wisdom of many who are able to age gracefully by keeping their mental capacities sharp.

Peaches has always been pretty pain tolerant unless she was afraid you wanted to meddle with her touchy areas. When Bentley hit her with his plastic baseball bat, she didn't bark. She liked to be underfoot when Glenda or I cook in the kitchen. Then she could pounce on any food we happened to drop—whether intentionally or not. She was so quiet while we focused on the cooking that sometimes we accidentally stepped on her. If only she made some noise, we would have avoided stepping on her. But she refrained from making any noise at all.

But Glenda and I have noticed lately that when we picked her up gently, she sometimes yelped. Her shoulders and upper back were much more sensitive than in the past. At ninety-eight, she felt the pain much more than before. Arthritis likely bothered her. She had some cysts around that same area that she did not have previously. Her back was arched a lot more than it used to be. We just knew she was uncomfortable in places where she wasn't before. We focused on giving love pats a little more softly than before because when we touched her neck and shoulders, she squawked.

She showed other evidence of aging. She slept more. Especially in the summer heat, she slowed down on our walks, and I had to carry her a short distance home. I remembered Autumn's observation that she had a hip out of alignment that slows her down when she walks. She didn't eat quite as much. All of the above were signs of aging that will just as easily slow down a person.

There were, however, still signs of health. Even though she was ninety-eight in dog years, I was amazed at how often a total stranger looked at her and said, "You have such a cute puppy."

One Friday, Peaches and I were walking on the sidewalk south of our house. A school bus stopped in the middle of the street beside us and let out a high school student. I waved to her; she waved back and then said, "You have a cute puppy."

I know you are not supposed to reveal a woman's age but didn't help myself. "She is fourteen years old," I informed her.

She was surprised because Peaches hid her age well. She still jumped up onto any of the three recliners we have. It may have taken a few more tries, but she didn't ever give up. She eventually accomplished her mission. She still jumped up into the car from the driveway. She still ate pretty well for her age. She still ran fast, racing pretty speedily at ninety-eight, to bark at the German shepherd who was going berserk behind the neighbor's fence.

Two days before her one-hundredth birthday, Peaches and I walked over a mile on our longest route. She was bouncy and raring to go. Her ears were flopping up and down as she hopped through the grass.

Peaches and I walked at least a mile every day, with a couple of exceptions. If the weather was cold or included recent rains, we walked half the route. If the weather was so bad there was no school or the heat index was over one hundred degrees, we didn't go. Period. We should all age so gracefully.

Bruce Fogle writes about how well poodles adjust to the aging process. He says, "Miniatures and Toys often reach 14 or 15 years. They often maintain their playfulness and physical dexterity well into their senior years."[1] In addition, the Maltese side of Peaches also maintained its zest into old age.

She still had her playfulness, just not as often. Rachel was the best at getting her to play. Peaches recovered very well from the illness that scared me recently. She was able to do all she did before she got sick. She showed more emotion than she did in her younger days. Glenda talked to Peaches with a lot more emotion than I do; Peaches sensed this emotion and wagged her tail for her. Peaches didn't wag her tail as much for me.

Peaches showed emotion in other ways: a moaning sound, a high-pitched purr almost like a kitten's, the spin cycle, barking, or licking. When Glenda asked for a kiss, Peaches licked Glenda on the nose. Peaches usually kissed me on the hand. I was OK with that, preferring she lick my hand, not my nose. Sometimes I didn't realize my hand was that close to her, and she surprised me with a kiss. What a lot of spunk and spirit this elderly dog still expresses!

Consider one little verse that tells a story about a biblical hero. "Moses was a hundred and twenty years old when he died, yet his eyes were not weak nor his strength gone" (Deut. 34:7).

Take notice of some of those people we all envy who get older but never look as if they have aged. There might be someone in your neighborhood. I think of people in the limelight who are old enough to be on social security—actors and actresses, models, singers. In no particular order: Christie Brinkley, Cher, Jane Fonda, Robert Redford, Jane Seymour. Even Rob Lowe doesn't look as if he could be in his fifties. Peaches was a dog's version of those forever-young people.

As Peaches added on more years, I had to encourage her even more with love pats and kisses on the top of her head. She needed more care and compassion than she did in the past.

The same kind of love is needed for elderly people who sit or lie in a nursing home all day. They are so lonely that they want their visitors, if they have any, to stay for a long time. They work at dominating the conversation because they know that as long as they are talking, it's harder for you to leave. They have paid their dues yet are often abandoned.

Although no nursing home could house a dog twenty-five years ago, it is pretty common today. Those live-in dogs and the dogs belonging to the nursing home staff offer residents friendship as their constant companions.

The apostle Paul offers some encouragement with his positive outlook. He writes, "Therefore we do not lose heart. Though outwardly wasting away, inwardly we are being renewed day by day" (2 Cor. 4:16).

David, the king and writer of Psalms, offers a prayer for the elderly that Peaches would like. It would have been sung by the Hebrews in the temple. David writes, "Even when I am old and gray, do not forsake me, my God, till I declare your power to the next generation, your mighty acts to all who are to come" (Ps. 71:18).

28

Empty Nesters

We appreciated Peaches when Glenda and I were both working full time. Actually, we were working time and a half when you add up the hours and stress of our jobs. It's a blessing the Maltese breed was ranked second of seven top breeds that excel in a family with full-time employees. They adjusted fine to the family's busy schedule.

Peaches had endured our move and been in our home for only three months when Andrea went off to the university to begin her freshman year. Rachel had graduated from college and was working in Kansas City. We were now officially empty nesters. Consequently, it was Peaches who softened the blow, who minimized our pain with both girls gone from home.

That would soon change during the coming year. A lucky penny always returns. Rachel decided to come back home because the "great" job she was working had an insurmountable problem. The owner was in over her head and could not pay her help. After weeks of waiting, we had to contact the Kansas Department of Labor for her paychecks to show up. Her move was also precipitated by her fiancé finding a teaching job in Wichita.

Andrea had gone off to college, and her grades were excellent, but she was not comfortable in the massive state university. It was just too big to suit her. She had taken classes at a different college for second semester but didn't enjoy that one either. She moved back home, checked into some other colleges, and the next fall enrolled at Southwestern College, where she graduated after just three total years in college, including her initial semester at the state university.

Rachel got married the next summer, and Andrea went off to college, so we got a second helping of living as empty nesters. Peaches was the catalyst again to soften the pain of our children moving on to the real world.

Wikipedia defines the empty nest in this way. "Empty nest syndrome is a feeling of grief and loneliness parents may feel when their children leave home for the first time, such as to live on their own or to attend college or university. It is not a clinical condition."[1] Whew! Glad to know it is not a clinical condition. They had me scared. According to Wikipedia's definition, the second time does not count as empty nest syndrome. Whoops! Sorry for trying to count the second time we were without children as making us empty nesters.

Should you be suffering from this nonclinical condition, you may be wondering what breed of dog works well for empty nesters. James Kelly has an answer in his article titled "The Right Dog: Outstanding Addition for 50+ Empty Nester or Older."[2] As anyone reaches retirement age, probably not relating to coworkers any more, it is common for loneliness to set in. A dog can offer unwavering love and loyalty. A dog can motivate the senior citizen to escape the house and walk for some exercise.

James Kelly also cites studies that reveal dogs have a positive effect on dementia. Kelly says, "Studies have found that dogs slow the process by which seniors with dementia lose their memory because they keep on a schedule and provide comfort when their owner is having a bad day or is distressed."[3]

The following nine breeds can fill the void in the empty nest as a therapy dog, the newest kid in the family, or a playmate to share some fun. The Yorkshire terrier serves as a great companion and a ferocious watchdog for seniors who are dealing with the loss of hearing. Labrador retrievers are the most popular breed of dog in the United States and Canada. They are frequently trained to help the blind, offer therapy, or assist law enforcement. Pomeranians are friendly, social dogs that are able to act as watchdogs.

Greyhounds can be low key when not in a race. They require lots of exercise and make great therapy dogs. Maltese dogs find ways to charm you into spoiling them and make a great match for a senior who is downsizing in a small apartment. The French bulldog has a sweet, calm nature and needs close contact with humans.

The Havanese breed forms a close bond with one person—a perfect match for a senior who lives alone. Poodles are intelligent, easy to train, hypoallergenic, and fun with their sense of humor. The Cairn terrier will do anything to please and enjoys being petted and receiving affection. The empty nester can find a compatible dog among these breeds.

In gratitude to the Mayo Clinic, I have taken an article they posted on the net about empty nesters and adapted it to serve those whose dog is no longer a part of the family. These mourners are missing the constant companionship of the dog they have loved so deeply.

On the positive side, studies have shown that new opportunities open up for these grieving folks. Now is a great time to reconnect with your spouse and to work on that relationship. Rebuild other relationships with friends or family. You can reinvent the time you devoted to your dog and spend it on previous interests and hobbies. Don't neglect the exercise you gained from walking your dog; now you need it more than ever as you cope. Perhaps it is time to go back to the gym or play golf or pickleball.

Good Morning America spotlighted a new study asserting that a dog in the home improves cardiovascular health.[4] It reminds us that once the dog is no longer in the home, more effort and intentionality to keep exercising are necessary.

Take positive action. Unfortunately, some people in your situation have become so arrested in their grief that all things spiral down out of control to a harsh, negative outlook. Those same people can succumb to depression, an identity crisis, alcoholism, or marital and familial conflict.

Do not be afraid to seek support from family, friends, and mental health professionals. Do not hold back on letting out those deep-seated emotions that come with any grief you feel. Do not worry about those people who think you are crazy to have loved a dog so much.

Remember that real grief takes time. Allow the extended time you need to experience a new comfort and peace. Only when you feel the heavy grief gradually fading away can you allow yourself to be prompted to look for a new dog.

Even if a dog costs more money than expected and requires more work than foreseen, that dog has enough love to bring joy to a home that no longer houses the younger generation. I cite another example: my Grandpa Roe. He was always on the road with his job as general superintendent of the Kansas Yearly Meeting of Friends, visiting many churches spread out over five states. His job was very similar to that of a bishop in other denominations. He took ten-week trips to the mission field in Burundi. Frankly, he wasn't home long enough to care for a dog.

When he retired to Haviland, Kansas, he found a dog whose breed resembled a ketchup company with fifty-seven varieties. He named the mutt Oscar. The dog looked as if some breed of terrier was predominant. He was a medium brown in color. Oscar added so much to the home and mindset of Merle and Ruth Roe, as a dog does for many retirees.

Oscar was spoiled by Grandpa and treated like one of the family. I remember hearing my grandfather's conversations with Oscar. He teased that dog, talking with him exactly as he talked to anyone else in the family. Oscar gave Grandpa a special presence in the home so he could share his love for the dog.

Grandpa was aware that another presence in the home was always around. I love a passage in Psalms that reminds us that God is always with us, that we cannot run from His presence. The psalmist writes,

Where can I go from your Spirit?

Where can I go from your presence?

If I go up to the heavens

You are there;

If I make my bed in the depths,

You are there.

If I rise on the wings of the dawn,

If I settle on the far side of the sea,

Even there your hand will guide me,

Your right hand will hold me fast. (Ps. 139:7–10)

The gist of this passage offers comfort to an empty nester. If you are living alone as a single person or as a retired couple, you cannot and will not escape the very presence of God. He is always with us.

Likewise, if you feel a void when the kids are gone, if you need a visible friend you can touch who will not argue with you, a dog can fill that void. We are not alone with man's best friend to provide constant companionship.

29

·· ● ··

Peaches' Dreams

Almost every night and sometimes multiple times, Peaches whimpered with a high-pitched moan. Not very loudly, but with a timid squeak recurring over and over. She dreamed pretty often. I usually gave her some love pats, and eventually she stopped the whimpering. Her entire body usually twitched as she made the whining noise. Both the sound and the jerking made me think her dreams were not too pleasant. I was convinced she most certainly dreamed. What pictures did she see in her dreams?

I wonder if her dreams are like mine. Allow me to share a dream that meant something to me. I am playing basketball with players who are much more talented than I am. I recognize some of the players who played for Kansas University, but none of them are superstars or in the NBA. I recognize the coach, whose name is Larry Brown.

I am playing the best defense of my life. Steals and stops without fouling. But I have blown it, missing three layups. I look to the bench, expecting Coach Brown to pull me, to offer me more pine time. I glance at the scorer's table, looking for a sub to confirm that my playing time is over. To my surprise, nobody is there, the empty table an affirmation that I will keep playing.

This dream happened when I was having some major issues at my job. It was as if God was saying, "Stay in the game. It will work out." There's a chance some players may have thought Brown played God, but the real message was from the God above.

God has spoken to me through dreams just as He did to the prophets. Numbers 12:6 reads, "He [God] said, 'Listen to my words: When there is a prophet among you, I, the Lord, reveal myself to them in visions, I speak to them in dreams." I have kept a journal of my dreams and can perceive some patterns in my dreams from the journal.

My dreams always appear in vivid pictures that include a familiar setting. Sometimes I know people in them; less often, I don't. Sometimes I am given names of people I eventually meet in the future. Often, God gives me a message that is so clear; it's not hard to understand. Sometimes God gives me direction on how to handle a situation, as in the dream above. Sometimes God brings to mind someone I hadn't thought about for some time and says, "This person needs help now. Go see him or her."

As I obey that guidance, I find that God is always right. You would be surprised at how many times I have heard, "How did you know I needed help?"

God uses my dreams to point out my sins. That usually happens when a snake appears in my dream. You will remember the serpent was the instrument of temptation and sin in the Garden of Eden. In one recurring dream, the snake is wrapped around my neck. I am struggling for life. It's as if God is saying, "That particular sin is killing you." And it is. God makes clear what the sin is and what I must do to eliminate it.

There are some dreams I am not sure how to interpret. Some of those go back for years, and I still ask, "God, what do you mean by this?" There are names of people I have never met that still stand out in my memory. Maybe I'll meet them in heaven.

And there are the weird dreams that make no sense to me. In one dream, I have stolen the car of a ninety-seven-year-old man so I can drive some kids to a church camp. I haven't bothered to tell the elderly man or his sons that I'm taking his car with ninety-seven thousand miles on it. I pray that the car doesn't break down, stranding the campers and me in the middle of nowhere. When we all return to the church, his sons are there, fidgeting, angry with me. I am trying to explain that my car wasn't functional, and the kids needed to arrive at camp.

Was I ever glad to wake up and realize it was only a dream! It didn't seem to relate to anything happening in my life. A direct message was not clear, but perhaps God was trying to highlight a sin I hadn't confessed.

But after spending some time reflecting on this dream, I find a couple of reminders from lessons learned in the past that are good to keep in mind. First, be sensitive to the needs of others. Don't ignore the feelings of the ninety-seven-year-old or his sons. This lesson keeps me from having to apologize later. Second, do not take more than your share in life. I cringe when my brothers remember that it was I who ate all the cookies and all the potato chips when we were kids. Duh, I understand the meaning of the dream. Don't steal your brothers' food!

Sometimes my mind wanders back to what Peaches may be dreaming. Why does she seem as if her dreams are so painful? Is she dreaming that I am accidently stepping on her again? Is a pit bull chasing her? Does she have beautiful dreams, too? I hope so, but I can't forget all the moaning and body jerking. Can she sit at the table and converse with her parents and family? Dream of heaven?

For those who may not be convinced that dogs dream, Stanley Coren, in his book *Do Dogs Dream?*, offers evidence that dogs do dream.[1] He mentions that Matthew Wilson and Kenway Louie of the Massachusetts Institute of Technology have shown that rats dream. A dog's brain is much more developed than that of a rat, so it is reasonable to believe that dogs dream. Wilson and Louie's test showed that the subject matter of a rat's dream originates from its daily activities, so it is likely the same for dogs.

Coren says, "The animal is certainly recalling memories of those events as they occurred during the awake state, and it is doing so during dream sleep, and that's just what people do when they dream."[2]

Coren points to research that suggests what some specific breeds might visualize in their dreams. He says, "Thus researchers found that a dreaming pointer may immediately start searching for game and may even go on point, a sleeping Springer Spaniel may flush an imaginary bird in his dreams, while a dreaming Doberman Pinscher may pick a fight with a dream burgular."[3]

But what do tiny lapdogs dream about? I hope Peaches dreams about a beautiful paradise called heaven. What in her daily activities would spark that dream? A daily walk. A doggy treat. Her loving family. Heavenly ice cream. We can't say for sure what Peaches dreams about, but we can be sure that little dogs dream more often than big dogs. Coren clarifies, "Not all dogs dream the same way. It is an odd fact that small dogs have more dreams than big dogs. A dog as small as a Toy Poodle may dream once every ten minutes, while a dog as large as a Mastiff or a Great Dane may have about an hour between dreams. The difference is that the big dog's dreams last longer."[4]

Just as my dreams appear in vivid living color and familiar settings, so do the dreams of some instrumental heroes of the Bible. Three times, an angel appears to the earthly father of Jesus in a dream. The first time, the angel tells Joseph not to be afraid to unite in marriage with Mary, for she is pregnant by the Holy Spirit. And the angel commands, "Name this child, the Son of God, Jesus" (Matt. 1:20–21). In the second dream, the angel says to stay in Egypt because the jealous Herod is killing baby boys (Matthew 2:13). Third, the angel says it is safe to go back home now (Matt. 2:19–20). God is guiding Joseph through these dreams.

Another Joseph, the one with the stupendous "technicolor dreamcoat," rises through the ranks of the Egyptian government because of his God-given skills at interpreting dreams. He asks, "Do not interpretations belong to God?" (Gen. 40:8).

Daniel has no trouble understanding dreams and visions. "And Daniel could understand dreams and visions of all kinds" (Dan. 1:17). In interpreting King Nebuchadnezzar's dream, Daniel gives proper credit for the interpretation. "But there is a God in heaven who reveals mysteries" (Dan. 2:28).

Elihu speaks some convincing words to his friend Job. He says, "For God does speak—now one way, now another—though no one perceives it. In a dream, in a vision of the night when deep sleep falls on people as they slumber in their beds, he may speak in their ears and terrify with warnings, to turn them from wrongdoing and keep them from pride, to preserve them from the pit, their lives from perishing by the sword" (Job 33:14–18).

After Peaches aged past 101 and slept through many naps each day, a new dreaming pattern emerged. She dozed on my lap and suddenly jumped out from under her blanket, acting alarmed and afraid. It has never been a part of her personality to be so scared. She got some altitude on those leaps, especially for her age. Peaches must have dreamed the pit bull down the street was closing in on her. The scary dreams happened numerous times—it's too bad the nightmares outnumbered dreams about ice cream beyond the pearly gates.

We have established that dogs dream, but as to the content of their dreams, we can do no more than speculate. From scripture and experience, it is evident that the God of the universe plays an active part in our dreams. Even though I asked Peaches what vivid pictures she saw in her dreams, she hasn't bothered to make that clear just yet.

"Peaches, what were you dreaming about last night when all the moaning and groaning was going on?" I asked.

Talking to my dog might have made me smarter than those who didn't, but it has never gotten that particular question answered. She was too quiet.

30

•• • ••

"Reverence for Life"

Talk about a jack-of-all-trades. Who could have found the time to serve effectively as an organist, theologian, writer, administrator, missionary, physician, surgeon, hospital founder, movie actor, philosopher, and pastor? If that's not enough on his resume, he also spent time in an internment camp as a prisoner of war.

Born January 14, 1875, in a small village in Alsace, then in Germany, Albert Schweitzer was innately blessed by some important influence from his ancestors. They excelled throughout many previous generations in Christian theology, music, and education. His father and maternal grandfather were pastors, both grandfathers were talented organists, and many among his family were scholars.[1]

When Albert Schweitzer was nine years old, he played the organ in his father's church before the entire congregation. He would later become talented enough to become an internationally known concert organist. From the money he made through concerts, he was able to pay for his education, including medical school, and the building of a hospital at Lambaréné in French Equatorial Africa, now Gabon.[2]

He studied rigorous, in-depth theology at the University of Strasbourg, earning a doctor of philosophy degree in 1899. That same year, he was ordained and began serving as the pastor at Saint

Nicholas Church in Strasbourg. He also served as an administrator at the Theological College of Saint Thomas in Strasbourg.

Strasbourg is on the border between France and Germany, along the Rhine River. Hence, the city has changed nationalities four times, alternating between the two countries. Albert Schweitzer was a citizen of Germany until 1919, when he became a citizen of France. Today, both the European Parliament and the Council of Europe are located in Strasbourg.

Schweitzer wrote seventeen books during his lifetime. He wrote a biography of Johann Sebastian Bach in French in 1905, a book on organ building and organ playing in 1906, and a rewrite of the Bach biography in German in 1908. He also wrote a book on theology titled *The Quest of the Historical Jesus* in 1906.

As a Lutheran, he challenged the secular view of Jesus and the traditional Christian understanding. That particular book caused quite a theological revolution, for it went against the grain of traditional beliefs. In another book, Schweitzer interpreted Paul's view of "being in Christ" as primary and "justification by faith" as secondary, contradicting Luther.

By 1905, he had decided to become a medical missionary instead of a pastor, so he started medical school, completing it in 1913. He also went back to Lambaréné and founded the hospital in 1913.

In the meantime, he had married Helene Bresslau, municipal inspector for orphans, in 1912. Her father, Harry Bresslau, was a Jewish German historian.

In 1917, Schweitzer and his wife, still citizens of Germany, became prisoners of war at a French internment camp. There was no trial to explore the possibility of freeing them. Released in 1918, they returned to Strasbourg for the next six years. During that time period, Albert Schweitzer preached at Saint Nicholas Church, gave concerts and teaching sessions, and took more medical classes.

In 1924, Albert and Helene returned to Lambaréné, where they would spend the rest of their lives. He gradually expanded the hospital to include seventy buildings that had the capacity to care for five hundred patients. In Lambaréné he would serve in many roles: surgeon, doctor, pastor of a church, administrator of a village, superintendent of buildings and grounds, writer of books, commentator on contemporary history, musician, and host to many visitors.

What did the man do in his spare time? He played Zirkus, an artist, in a movie titled *Bimbo the Great* in 1958. A previous biographical documentary released November 22, 1957 won an Academy Award for Best Documentary Feature in America. A later movie about his life, titled *Albert Schweitzer*, posthumously premiered on Christmas Eve of 2009.

In 1952, Albert Schweitzer was presented with the Nobel Peace Prize as a result of his philosophy of "Reverence for Life." Schweitzer did not receive the monetary reward of $33,000 for the Nobel Prize until 1953. He used that money to build a hospital wing for lepers.

His philosophy of "Reverence for Life" was influenced by a principle originating in India called Jainism, or nonviolence, before Mahatma Gandhi lived out that doctrine. In short, "Reverence for Life" is a respect, admiration, and high regard for all God's creatures.

In his book *Civilization and Ethics*, Schweitzer writes, "Respect for life, overcoming coarser impulses and hollow doctrines, leads the individual to live in the service of other people and every living creature."[3]

Schweitzer also defined the purpose of a person's life. He said, "The purpose of human life is to serve, and to show compassion and the will to help others."[4] All his service, scads of jobs, and accomplishments showed he practiced these words.

Albert Schweitzer explained the road to peace. He said, "Until he extends his circle of compassion to include all living things, man will not himself find peace."[5] Perhaps Peaches gave thanks she was included in Schweitzer's quote above.

Following are some quotations from scripture that reinforce Schweitzer's quotations on "Reverence for Life." Job 12:7–10 says, "But ask the animals, and they will teach you, or the birds in the sky, and they will tell you; or speak to the earth, and it will teach you, or let the fish in the sea inform you. Which of all these does not know that the hand of the Lord has done this? In his hand is the life of every living creature and the breath of all mankind." The animals can teach us so much. In considering my time with Peaches, I am sure that she has taught me a lot, as this passage proclaims.

The Bible tells us of the importance of taking care of the animals. It says, "The godly take care of their animals, but the wicked are always cruel" (Prov. 12:10, New Living Testament).

Scripture tells us that even the wild animals honor God. Isaiah 43:20 says, "The wild animals honor me, the jackals and the owls, because I provide water in the wilderness and streams in the wasteland, to give drink to my people, my chosen."

Albert Schweitzer passed away on September 4, 1965, and was buried in Lambaréné, where he had served in a multitude of ways, giving that community his heart of compassion.

Albert Schweitzer made lots of major sacrifices to make sure the ill and impoverished were taken care of in Africa. He could have followed any of his talents and education to a career that would have been much more lucrative. He used the prize money from the Nobel Peace Prize not for his own gain but to provide medical care for lepers. After being imprisoned as a prisoner of war, he came back to Strasbourg, but during his time there he was preparing to travel back to Africa.

Once he came back to Lambaréné six years later, he served there for the rest of his remaining life. No one can give more in a multitude of ways to serve. He pointed out what a priority it is that we value all living creatures.

Peaches may have appreciated Schweitzer's worldview. All living creatures can be thankful for his teachings.

31

•••

A Dog's Grief

At one o'clock in the morning, Glenda and I were awakened by a phone call from our nephew. Our brother-in-law, Choc, had passed away unexpectedly. He lived alone, so there was no telling how long he had been dead. Choc was given his nickname by his school buddies because he always chose chocolate ice cream at the drug store. Choc was quite a legend on the basketball court, once scoring fifty-two points in a high school game before there was such a thing as a three-point line.

Choc loved Kansas Jayhawk basketball but hated Duke. Duke had lost the evening before his death. When his son did not get a phone call to celebrate Duke's loss, Curtis began to wonder what was going on. That's when he drove thirty miles from Salina, Kansas, to McPherson to check on Choc.

Glenda and I also worked at opening our eyes at that ungodly hour. We threw grody clothes on and drove ninety miles to McPherson in middle-of-the-night silence. Because of the shock of his death and trying to awaken, we rode in quietness most of the way. With our eyes still barely open and pasted toward the windshield, we talked a little, trying to process our pain, our shock, our grief. We journeyed over pitch-black roads that matched our pain and shock. Mentally, emotionally, we couldn't deal with it.

When we arrived at Choc's house, just north of McPherson College, Stockman Mortuary had already shown up. Choc was lying on the bed with his faithful Pomeranian, Tasha, beside him. Tasha was their second Pomeranian, following Chi Chi. There's no telling how long Tasha had been able to keep from wetting on the carpet, but once we arrived, she could wait no longer. Glenda was quick to clean it up.

We watched as the morticians loaded Choc onto the gurney. As they wheeled the gurney into the living room, Tasha tried to jump up on the gurney just before they exited out the front door. Tasha's jump did not reach the top of the gurney, so she tried again. No success. I will never forget that graphic picture of Tasha wanting to be with her master, a memory of her loyalty and companionship. She wasn't ready to let go of Choc.

Yet Tasha's story became even more tragic. Curtis had a toy poodle, and he knew his dog had never accepted Tasha. There would never be room for both dogs in his house. Within a couple of days, Curtis sold Tasha. Not only did she have to go through grief and mourning with no one from the family she loved around to support her, but she also had to adjust to a new owner.

Tasha knew Choc was dead. She understood. She had lain on the bed with Choc for many hours, receiving no response. Her effort to keep from wetting on the carpet was a sign of her loyalty to Choc. Her jumps to accompany Choc on the gurney demonstrate that she was already grieving.

Dogs surely go through grief just as we humans do. The example of Hachi in chapter 12 supports that idea. Hachi continued to look for his deceased owner at the train station every afternoon for nine years after his master had passed away. Dogs hurt just as we do when their masters die.

Matt Roper reports a story—similar to Hachi's—of a black German shepherd from Argentina.[1] Miguel Guzman bought the dog, Capitan, as a present for his thirteen-year-old son, Damian. Soon after Miguel's death, Capitan went missing. A week after Miguel Guzman passed away, his family went to his grave to pay their respects. There they found the heartbroken dog sitting at his master's grave, wailing.[2] The loyal Capitan slept at the grave in Villa Carlos Paz near Córdoba until his death eleven years later.

In an article from the American Kennel Club, Alexandra Anastasio attempts to answer the question "Do Dogs Grieve the Loss of Their Human Owners?" Her brief answer says, "It's not unusual for dogs to grieve the loss of a person they've bonded with who is no longer present."[3] She goes on to say there are specific signs to look for after a dog's loss, including panting, whining, barking, pacing, and fidgeting.[4]

Dogs grieve in different ways and time patterns, just as humans do.

The dog's owner should watch for indicators affecting a dog's health. These may be any combination of a loss of energy, sluggishness, clinginess, loss of interest in physical activity, and loss of appetite resulting in weight loss.[5]

In June of 2014, Constable Dave Ross, a Canadian general duty officer and police dog handler, lost his life while working on the job. His service dog, a German shepherd named Danny, had worked beside him during his time as an officer. During the entire length of Ross's funeral, the loyal Danny whimpered beside his master's casket.[6]

Jamie Thomas is executive director of Motley Zoo Animal Rescue in Redmond, Washington. She says, "Dogs are highly intuitive and sensitive."[7]

Author Anastasio says, "Dogs do understand the emotional feeling of missing someone who's no longer a part of their daily lives."[8]

Barbara J. King is a professor of anthropology at the College of William and Mary and author of the book *How Animals Grieve*. She says, "Grief can be said to occur when a survivor animal acts in ways that are visibly distressed or altered from the usual routine, in the aftermath of the death of a companion animal who had mattered emotionally to him or her."[9]

How can we help the grieving dog recover? Anastasio suggests five steps. "Be aware of routines and try to stick to them. Provide comfort by spending more time together. Give extra affection—touch increases your bond. Play the dog's favorite game. Increase exercise."[10]

Anastasio says, "With time, most dogs recover emotionally."[11] Good news!

As our dogs grieve, we realize they have an even greater need for our love and support. The above signs of their grieving remind us that although dogs cannot talk, they communicate with us in many other ways. All four of the stories of dogs in mourning above emphasize the high level of grief dogs endure.

Surely the following passages of scripture apply to dogs, just as they do to humans. Psalm 147:3 says, "He [God] heals the brokenhearted and binds up their wounds."

And Lamentations 3:32 comforts us: "Though he [God] brings grief, he will show compassion, so great is his unfailing love."

We are not able to know whether dogs journey through Elizabeth Kubler-Ross's five stages of grief—denial, anger, bargaining, depression, and acceptance—but we can be sure they pass through intense grief. The intensity of their grief is displayed in the faithful loyalty to their masters they show—going so far as to lie beside their graves or familiar posts for days, months, and years.

32

•• ● ••

People Left Behind

What is the hardest thing about owning a dog? The goodbye. I will never forget the stomach cancer that was making our sheltie, Lady Luck, suffer. Even more difficult to forget is the look of pain and confusion in her eyes before Glenda took her to the vet to be euthanized. No longer was there any chance of her recovering. We had had to say goodbye to Lacey, our Chihuahua, six months earlier. Painful as it was, we had to journey through the agony of mourning our loss.

The unlikely positive in that process was that their deaths jump-started our purchase of Peaches. She helped to fill the void left behind by the deaths of the other two dogs, even though we missed Lady and Lacey. Some people may refer to them as just dogs, but that's not how we feel when we grieve our loss.

Peaches has been my constant companion. Crushed was how I would have felt when she was no longer in our house each day. Peaches remained loyal and never argued with me, made fun of me, or told me I was crazy.

Dogs become just as much a part of our family as humans. Sandra Barker, director of the Center for Human-Animal Interaction at Virginia Commonwealth University, coauthored a study that proves just how close animals are in our families. Joe Yonan refers to Barker's study in an article in the *New York Post*.

Yonan writes, "Researchers have long known that the animal-human bond is strong: A 1988 study in the *Journal of Mental Health Counseling* asked a group of dog owners to place symbols for their family members and pets in a circle representing each dog owner's life. (The distance between the subject and the other symbols corresponds to the relative, real-life closeness of those relationships.)"

Yonan continues, "The subjects tended to put the dog closer than the average family member, and about as close as the closest family member; in 38% of the cases, the dog was closest of all."[1]

Sometimes humans find it difficult to accept that it is all right to grieve over a loved pet. Yet it is normal to grieve over a pet. Many people are surprised when they discover feelings suggesting it is as difficult to lose a pet as a human. The title of Yonan's article above doesn't hide his feelings: "The Death of a Pet Can Hurt As Much As the Loss of a Relative."[2]

Yonan shares the agony he felt over the death of his dog. He says, "It's been four months and yet if somebody asks me about that day, my voice will crack...I came home from work to find my Doberman, Red, splayed out on my bedroom floor...his body lifeless but still warm. It's an image I can't seem to shake."[3]

Barker said her clients are alarmed they are grieving more for their pets than for a sibling or relative. She says, "But when they realize that the difference is the pet gave them constant companionship, and there was total dependency, then they start to realize that's why they're grieving so intensely."[4]

Adam Clark in *Psychology Today* agrees. He says, "Research shows us that grieving the death of our companion animals can be just as painful, if not more than, grieving the loss of a family member or friend."[5]

In an article titled "Losing a Pet Is Much More Painful Than Most People Think," published in *Science* magazine, Mark Breitenberg offers more evidence about the difficulty of mourning a pet. He says, "Hawaiian researchers have also initiated some studies into the pain felt after losing a pet and interestingly, they have even found that the pain after the death of a pet is usually much longer lasting than the pain which is felt after the loss of a loved one."[6]

He goes even further on the subject. Breitenberg says, "Losing them is like losing their soul mate."[7]

Our experts all agree. If you have ever felt the deep pain of losing a pet, you would likely agree with these experts. Yet I know of another group who would not go quite so far about the pain of an animal's death. Widows and widowers whom I have talked to are fully aware of how deeply the pain stabs at one's heart when a spouse of forty, fifty, or sixty years passes away. That relationship has lasted a lot longer than a dog's entire life span. That group of mourners would have trouble agreeing that their grief does not last as long as the grief over a dog.

Similarly, parents whose child precedes them in death do not ever get over it. My friends Jim and Priscilla Pykiet suffered through the death of their eighteen-year-old daughter, Becky. One of Rachel's teachers in Vacation Bible School, Becky was greatly loved by her classmates. After a night on the town, three friends were in a car with a drunk driver who sped down Oliver Street in Wichita at over one hundred miles an hour, colliding with a tree just south of Central Street. Becky was one of two others in that car who lost their young lives. Only one survived. For one entire day I served as a counselor to busloads of high school students who came to the mortuary crying their eyes out.

Thirty years later, Jim cannot talk about it without tears. Yet he has gone so far as to serve as an advocate in court for many people who have suffered as victims or loved ones of drunk drivers. Jim has been able to utilize his grief to help others going through similar pain. What an amazing example of compassion and comfort!

Veterinarians grieve when they run out of options to keep a dog alive. Dr. Brenda Gough from Brantford, Ontario, after having to euthanize a dog she had known since it was a puppy, shared on Facebook the pain she felt as she "sobbed hysterically." She said, "I want her to live forever for you. I want that so badly it hurts. I feel like I have failed her and you when I have run out of options to keep them and you comfortable and happy."[8]

As the family's vet, she loved the privilege of watching the kids grow up and feeling like a part of the family's journey. Gough says this:

"How your vet sees euthanasia…

"So you bring me this puppy—she kisses my face, devours the cookies I offer, and our friendship starts.

"Several visits later, he starts to learn where all the cookie jars are in the clinic, and that lady in the white coat, well, she's okay."[9]

Gough has by then come to love the dog and the family. She received over twenty-eight thousand grateful comments for her honesty from social media users. One person commented, "Over my lifetime there have been several and my heart has broken every time! I thank my vet for always making it a little easier."

Another wrote, "So well written and so honest. Tears are running down my face."

It is acceptable and necessary to grieve deeply over the death of a dog. You should never feel guilty or ashamed about your grieving for a dog. Tears are not anything to run from while you're grieving over a beloved dog, but you may have days when you can't stop the tears, no matter how hard you try. Mama said there'd be days like that, and Mama said not to feel bad about it. It simply shows the depth of your love for a dog, for which you do not have to apologize. Over the long haul, tears bring healing.

Most of us have a scheduled routine with our dogs—when we take a walk, when we feed them, when we let them outside. Memories will come back during those times in your day, and the memories take us back to the grief. Grief can be even more intense over a dog who has worked beside you, such as a guide dog for the blind or a drug-sniffing dog with an officer.

When I was a child, most of my school buddies thought it was a big joke to have a funeral for an animal. But it wasn't funny when it was their family dog. Yet some folks seem embarrassed to think we could pay our respects to an animal with a funeral as we do for humans. Just as a funeral is an essential element of the mourning process for a human, it works the same way for a dog. In addition, a family gathering where family members tell stories of their dog helps in the grieving process.

We have friends who lost their fourteen-year-old Yorkie in the most painful way. The father let the dog out at six thirty in the morning when it was still dark. Then he watched as a coyote swooped in and took off with the defenseless victim. There was no warning and no way to prevent it. Dad, Mom, and four children were devastated in an instant. It wasn't long before they found a new puppy to add to the family.

Many times, I have witnessed people who stayed frozen in denial. They found ways to stay busy so they didn't have to deal with the grief. It is never healthy when people attempt to short-circuit the mourning process, regardless of whether the grief is for humans or animals. Deep-seated problems rise to the surface later on. Journeying through the mourning process to keep ourselves healthy is one way we could honor Schweitzer's "Reverence for Life."

Lindsey, our sable-and-white sheltie, ran away from home. We gave our complete selves to searching for our eleven-year-old dog but never saw her again. We grieved our loss and found it a challenge to find a sense of closure.

Warning: a deeply personal story follows. In so many ways, Dad was an exceedingly upright man. At night, he would direct our family to kneel down on the carpeted floor in the living room and say our prayers. That's how I learned that even with a carpet, the floor doesn't feel any softer after you are on your knees for a long time. He influenced lots of youth as a junior high guidance counselor, coach, and summer recreation director. He made sure I got the chemistry set I wanted for Christmas.

He served our country in the South Pacific during World War II, a challenging task that never came up in his conversation. He financially supported people of other cultures, people who were in great need. He taught Sunday school and never missed church. He was sociable with many people. I never heard him say one swear word. When it came time for him to take up residency in a nursing home, he asked for one thing. His Bible.

He set a great example, yet one thing was lacking to this son: words of affirmation. OK, he did mention to my brothers he liked my form on a jump shot.

Our pastor and his wife, Jim and Jeanne Pitts, went as counselors to the high school church camp where I remember pitching on a baseball team. The next week, they told Dad they were proud of me. Dad relayed their message to me but didn't add his own affirmation.

Many years later, Father's Day was approaching, and I picked out a card and mailed a lengthy letter with it. I wrote about how appreciative I was for the role model he had been. The letter communicated my love for him. Yet I got no response. I could only assume he had received it.

After Dad passed away, my sister, Patricia, spent lots of time going through his possessions. She sent me two items he had kept for over twenty-five years. One was a news clipping picturing the class with which I was ordained. It was safe to assume he must have been proud that his son became a pastor.

The other was the Father's Day card and the letter expressing my love. It meant something special that he kept the card for so many years. Only then did I know he had received it and liked it.

As with many fathers of Dad's generation, saying "I love you" was not how he was brought up, nor was it verbalized. Dad, however, did write those three important words in a birthday card. They were the same words absent for countless hurting souls sitting in the counselee's seat across from me, their eyes overflowing freely with tears during our counseling sessions. Robert Bly classifies it as "father hunger."

To overcome that memory, I try to remember that Dad worked really hard to provide for his family. I resolve all this by remembering ways Dad showed love to me. It wasn't that he didn't love me. But I needed a few more words of affirmation.

The moral is as plain as any message from the red lights and siren approaching in the rearview mirror. Don't wait until after they are gone—whether humans or pets—to express our appreciation and love.

Grieving the loss of a loved one, including a pet, is a long process that—oh so slowly-- leads to comfort after a lengthy time of mourning.

Jesus said, "Blessed [or 'happy'] are those who mourn, for they shall be comforted" (Matt. 5:4).

The more deeply we love, the more deeply we mourn. And the more we mourn, the more we need comfort from loved ones and from God. II Corinthians 1:3–5 reads, "Praise be to the God and Father of our Lord Jesus Christ, the Father of compassion and the God of all comfort, who comforts us in all our troubles, so that we can comfort those in any trouble with the comfort we ourselves receive from God. For just as we share abundantly in the sufferings of Christ, so also our comfort abounds through Christ."

Comfort stands out as the theme of this passage, as the word is used five times in the verses above and four more times in the next two verses. Comfort begins with God. Praise God for that comfort. Yet we are asked to share that comfort with those who need it, and we receive comfort through those who share it. Comfort abounds.

For all the mourning and pain from a potpourri of different breeds that I mourned, God was able to provide the comfort needed.

Jesus said, "You will grieve, but your grief will turn to joy" (John 16:20b).

Dean Koontz, who had already written twenty number one *New York Times* bestsellers, writes about the pain of mourning Trixie, a Golden retriever, in his book *A Big Little Life: A Memoir of a Joyful Dog Named Trixie*.[10] Trixie had belonged to the Koontz family after retiring at the age of three from working as a Canine Companions for Independence service dog.

Dean and his wife, Gerda, were lost after Trixie passed away at the age of twelve. Koontz describes the funk they endured. He writes that he had never had writer's block before—a believable statement after his twenty bestsellers—but he could not type one word on his screen for the next three weeks.

Then out of the blue came a sign of comfort. Together, Dean and Gerda walked the two and a half acres Trixie had loved. Koontz says, "Three weeks to the minute after Trixie died...a brilliant golden butterfly swooped down from a pepper tree. This was no butterfly like any we had seen before; nor have we seen it since. Big, bigger than my hand when I spread my fingers, it was bright gold, not yellow."[11]

The butterfly touched their faces and then disappeared into thin air.

"Was that Trixie?" Gerda asked.

"Yeah, it was," Dean replied.

Dean and Gerda agreed that the butterfly's wings were different from anything they had seen before. Gerda recalled the wings were "almost edged in a neon rope."[12] Dean observed that the wings were too thick to fly and looked like stained glass with a leaded edge.

"Skeptics will wince, but I will always believe our girl wanted us to know that the intensity of our grief wasn't appropriate, that she was safe and happy,"[13] Koontz said.

Then readers of his website responded. "After sharing this on my Web site, I received hundreds of letters from readers who, after losing beloved dogs, experienced uncanny events that were quite different from ours but that seemed to be intended to tell them that the spirits of their dogs lived on,"[14] said Koontz.

"Like a mother comforts her child, so I will comfort you," God says in Isaiah 66:13. I see a vivid picture of a young mother bending down to her child's level, arms embracing her daughter, wanting to dry her tears and lift her spirit. This photo portrays exactly what the "God of all comfort" offers us.

Slowly, gradually, as if we were watching sand sift through an hourglass, we feel positive feelings edge up to overcome the pain. A. A. Milne writes these consoling words, said by Winnie the Pooh: "How lucky I am to have something that makes saying goodbye so hard."

"As a mother comforts her children, so I (God) will comfort you" (Isa. 66:13).

33

•• • ••

Kind Dogs in Heaven

In our living room hangs a beautiful painting I would love for you to see. Painted by Jim Warren, it is titled *All Dogs Go to Heaven*. A small boy sits on the grass, looking out to sea. In the center of the picture is a stone stairway to heaven that is lined by blue and red flowers—the rainbow bridge. In the sky are clouds; hidden in the clouds are ten different breeds of dogs, painted in sepia tones. At the bottom of the stairs is a dog facing us that looks just like Peaches. Perhaps the direction she faces hints that she is not quite ready to go up to heaven. Anyway, I hope she isn't quite ready for that yet. You can view this beautiful picture on the net.

Supposedly, Jim Warren got lots of complaints about this first edition of *All Dogs Go to Heaven*. The problem? Lots of people said, "My dog's not in the picture."

Jim Warren went back to work and gradually painted four more editions of the painting, showing other breeds. He also painted another picture called *All Cats Go to Heaven*. Warren painted three more on acrylic, picturing dogs in the water. Another of his paintings pictures horses running down a mountain with snow in the background.

Let's now contemplate an important question, especially for dog lovers. Do all dogs go to heaven?

To answer that question, the scriptures tell us that not even all people go to heaven. In speaking of those who don't help the needy, Jesus says, "Then they will go away to eternal punishment, but the righteous to eternal life" (Matt. 25:46).

Jesus also says, "Anyone who says, 'You fool!' will be in danger of the fire of hell" (Matt. 5:22). It surely sounds as if Jesus was convinced there is a hell. Some will continue to say, "No way," or "Prove it." My hope is that those people avoid the experience by coming to believe in the love of Jesus Christ.

Considering the 4.5 million dog bites each year in this country, some dogs may not reach heaven's gates. It follows that if not all people enter heaven, as Jesus says, not all dogs will make it to heaven. But throughout this book, we have witnessed lots of dogs who surely will find their reward in heaven.

King Solomon noticed a contrast in how people treat others. He says, "Those who are kind benefit themselves, but the cruel bring ruin on themselves" (Prov. 11:17). Solomon knew that different attributes in character led to results at opposing poles. Just as it is true for humans, this truth could also affect dogs in the same way.

Peter the apostle talks about a coming judgment day. He gives a justifiable reason Jesus Christ has not returned to earth for the Second Coming yet. Peter says, "The Lord is not slow in keeping his promise, as some understand slowness. Instead he is patient with you, not wanting anyone to perish, but everyone to come to repentance" (2 Pet. 3:9).

God does not want anyone to perish. Paul is another one who points to God's kindness as a means to bring us to repentance. Paul says, "God's kindness is intended to lead you to repentance" (Rom. 2:4).

Likewise, the psalmist lifts up God's goodness. He sings, "But you, Lord, are a compassionate and gracious God, slow to anger, abounding in love and faithfulness" (Ps. 86:15).

Some people may not believe heaven actually exists, and it took Dr. Eben Alexander seven days in a coma to be convinced it does. He is a neurosurgeon with decades of training. He has taught at medical schools including Duke, Harvard, and the Universities of Massachusetts and Virginia. He was trained to think in a scientific way. He could always find a rational reason to explain away all the stories he heard about people who had a "near-death" experience, who visited heaven. He did not believe their talk about heaven.

But then Dr. Alexander battled *E. coli* bacteria that were eating his brain away. During the time he was in the coma for seven days, he went through his own "life-after-life" experience with a wonderful view of heaven. He found out the music in heaven is immensely melodic and harmonic, beyond any dimension we have heard on earth. It's as if the music reaches a new dimension. Think the Trans-Siberian Orchestra times seven, on a higher plane, multiplied in intensity and beauty. Or music surpassing the Carpenters' Christmas CD.

Alexander is now sure heaven is real, and wrote a book called *Proof of Heaven*. In the book, he speaks of a message he received in three parts in heaven. The message said the following:

"You are loved and cherished, dearly, forever."

"You have nothing to fear."

"There is nothing you can do wrong."[1]

A former pastor-turned-seminary-professor told our class, "When you officiate at a funeral, it's not your job to put people in heaven or hell. That's up to God." I listened to the second part about hell, but when someone was a faithful saint and everyone knew it, we celebrated that.

This book has shared the stories of lots of dogs who deserve to go to heaven. For the kindness, companionship, and loyalty they have given to us humans, those dogs are worthy of the place Dr. Alexander has described. They have done things that are wrong, but so have we. As the seminary professor stressed, that's not up to me—only God can answer the question of heaven or hell.

I am convinced that there are many scriptures that point to animals in heaven. The chapters about Francis of Assisi and Albert Schweitzer have supplied a number of passages from the Bible that offer an affirmation of heaven for animals. Psalm 150:6 reads, "Let everything that has breath praise the Lord!" That text would include animals who praise God on earth, but it could just as easily embrace their praise in heaven, too.

Romans 8:19–21 also points to all creation. It reads, "For the creation waits in eager expectation for the children of God to be revealed. For the creation was subjected to frustration, not by its own choice, but by the will of the one who subjected it, in hope that the creation itself will be liberated from its bondage to decay and brought into the freedom and glory of the children of God." When the text emphasizes creation that is "liberated from bondage to decay," it includes the animals, as well as pointing to heaven.

The most concrete evidence is found in John's vision of heaven (Rev. 4:1–11). On the isle of Patmos, the "beloved disciple" sees four living creatures surrounding God's throne. Beginning in verse seven,

we read, "The first living creature was like a lion, the second was like
an ox, the third had a face like a man, the fourth was like a flying
eagle." The word "like" here can be understood in different ways, but
for me it's close enough to my favorite interpretation: "Yay! There
already are animals in heaven!"

That same John has a tremendous vision of what we can look
forward to in heaven (Rev. 21:1–4). He writes,

> Then I saw 'a new heaven and a new earth,' for the
> first heaven and the first earth had passed away, and
> there was no longer any sea. I saw the Holy City, the
> new Jerusalem, coming down out of heaven from
> God, prepared as a bride beautifully dressed for her
> husband. And I heard a loud voice from the throne
> saying, Look! God's dwelling place is now among
> the people, and he will dwell with them. They will
> be his people, and God himself will be with them
> and be their God. He will wipe every tear from their
> eyes. There will be no more death or mourning or
> crying or pain, for the old order of things has passed
> away.

No, the creatures are not mentioned in this passage. But "no more
death" could be the same as being "liberated from bondage to decay."
"No more mourning" reminds us that we have already established
that dogs mourn, too. I have no proof of heaven for animals, except
for what I read in the scriptures and what I hope for in my heart. Plus,
I am not the only one who wants to see our beloved pets in heaven.

No, the Bible does not explicitly say that there is a place for animals in heaven. But the Bible does imply there is. The Bible does

not say that animals have souls. Maybe that's where our faith rises up and says they do. Jennifer Skiff, in her book *The Divinity of Dogs: True Stories of Miracles Inspired by Man's Best Friend*, points out her belief that dogs do have souls. She writes, "I am among the ranks of millions of people who appreciate the souls of dogs and know they are a gift of pure love and an example of all that is good."[2]

A discussion between a vet and his client in England provides clarity concerning the souls of dogs. In his book *All Creatures Great and Small*, veterinarian James Herriot consoles an elderly client named Miss Stubbs.[3] Her Sealyham terrier, Ben, had just recently passed away. Miss Stubbs had but one fear; she told Herriot she would not see Ben when she soon passed away.

"They say animals have no souls," Miss Stubbs bemoaned.

"Who says?" asked Herriot.

"Oh, I've read it and I know a lot of religious people believe it."

"Well, I don't believe it. If having a soul means being able to feel love and loyalty and gratitude, then animals are better off than a lot of humans. They teach us vets all about animals' souls."

Miss Stubbs glowed, a look of relief covering her face, and snickered, her morale lifted to a new level.

Herriot responded, "I do believe it with all my heart."[4]

Scripture implies that a day will come when Peaches will be able to meet Chico, Taco, Tina, Gretchen, Lindsey, Lady Luck, Lacey, Oscar, and a host of other dogs. We can't leave out Scooter, Belle, Odin, Capitan, Hachi, Bella, Sadie, Canelo, Danny, Roselle, Millie, and Nova. Add in Suzy, Kramer, Charm, Buck, and Ellie. Even Lassie and Rin Tin Tin. Guide dogs, service dogs, war dogs, K-9 drug-sniffing dogs, and rescue dogs will surely receive a much-deserved ticket. This world is a brighter place because of them, and their next residence in heaven will be too.

I enjoy visualizing Peaches across the rainbow bridge, strutting her spin cycle in heaven. It's been my privilege to witness many people who, on their deathbeds, had no fear but were sure of a place in heaven. They had lived their days to the fullest, with a faith proclaiming there is nothing to fear. Now, as a dog owner, I have nothing to fear for her in the afterlife. She will be overwhelmed by love and care after her death.

That dog sneaked up on me, as I found a gradual, growing love for her after feeling dead set against taking her in when Andrea brought her home. I never asked to be the parent of a dog. I didn't expect to fill that role. But I found out it was an honor to be Dad for Peaches. I never lost an argument with her. She just agreed with me. She lived out the words of George Eliot. "Animals are such agreeable friends—they ask no questions, they pass no criticisms," said Eliot.

I wasn't always her shadow the way she was mine. She couldn't stand to eat alone, and sometimes she would allow her stomach to rumble with hunger before she would eat. I got busy with trivial tasks, and she would wait longer. My busyness kept her from eating. She did a better job of following me around than I did her, even though I made sure she had food and water.

My first impression of Peaches wasn't the best, but my lasting impression will always be imprinted on my mind, a picture of my shadow, who always stayed with me through beautiful days and challenging days. She has shown me enough love to remind me that first impressions don't have to last forever.

I see her in a different light now. She showed up to follow me wherever I went. She gradually morphed into my shadow. I couldn't have had a better dog for a buddy. I love that dog. I hang on to the hope of heaven for an aging Peaches and other kind dogs..

Epilogue

•• ● ••

Peaches has always been a morning person—er, dog. She celebrated her one-hundredth birthday by sleeping until nine thirty in the morning. I don't remember her ever sleeping in that late. She got to celebrate the centennial birthday with family—Glenda, Kevin, Rachel, Bentley, Scooter, and I. Andrea phoned from Omaha to wish Peaches a happy birthday.

We all signed a card picturing a caramel-colored Chihuahua with its tongue hanging out. The cover read, "Max wants to be the first to wish you a happy birthday." Inside it read, "He also wants to be the first to lick your face after you eat cake and ice cream. Happy birthday!"

Max missed out on the ice cream cake, but Peaches and the rest of us filled in for him for the difficult task of devouring it. Peaches seemed to appreciate a couple of small presents she received: a pink collar, size extra extra small, and a green hippopotamus squeaky toy. We sang "Happy Birthday"—though Bentley sang "Happy birthday to me."

She still has the desire to walk every day. She walked our longest route of a mile on the two days preceding her birthday. Peaches was lively, bouncing along through the grass, ears flopping. On her birthday, she seemed tired, and for that reason we walked the shortest route of a half mile. She was dragging, ambling along. She stopped at every opportunity, looking for an excuse to keep from going anywhere. She moseyed down the sidewalk. She was not nearly as spirited as she had been the two days before. But it still met my approval; after all, she can celebrate her hundredth birthday any way she wants.

What a recovery she made! The next three days, we were back to the longest route. Her legs had the former spring to them. Again, I remembered the words of her groomer, Autumn, who said, "She is still pretty spry."

On our walk, Peaches and I heard the usual comment. We met families leaving the playground on the sidewalk: three mothers, three little boys, and two toddler girls in strollers. One mother looked at Peaches and said, "She's so cute."

Later that afternoon, I laid down on the floor with Bentley for his nap time. Peaches went by me, making sure she did not touch me in a rough way but just barely brushed me. She was reminding me not to give all the attention to Bentley: "Don't forget about me."

She still cared about receiving my attention. She still had an appetite and ate nearly as much as she did in the past. She heard us better than Glenda and I heard each other. As I drove into the driveway today, Peaches heard the garage door open, went to the door, and barked. Glenda said she didn't hear anything. Positive notes for which we were thankful.

Peaches, however, showed signs of aging. She was slowing down. She had those days when she was not a bundle of energy on our walks. Her eyesight was not quite as clear as it used to be, as it took her longer to spot a treat on the floor. She slept more. She clung to me more closely. Peaches was still mentally sharp, but she sometimes stood in the middle of the driveway for an extended time, acting as if she didn't know what to do next. She was more unsure of herself and intermittently shook, with seemingly no ability to stop. We conceded these were all signs of her age, but we were grateful that she was as healthy as she was.

Even with all the aging signs so prevalent, Glenda and I set out on a road trip that we had planned six months earlier. Ten days, nine states, 2,953 miles. Kevin and Rachel were anxious about keeping Peaches in her elderly condition. Aware that she was not as lively as she had been six months earlier, we felt some misgivings ourselves. It didn't help our dilemma as we watched Peaches shaking violently during the ten-minute drive to their house.

Still, we ventured on to stay with Andrea and Jeff in Omaha, cherishing our time with six-month-old Hartley, loving her compelling smile and contagious laugh. We navigated on through Iowa to South Dakota, stopping at Wall Drug, Mount Rushmore, Keystone, Deadwood, and Sturgis. We marveled at a fifty-foot statue titled *Dignity*, crafted by Dale Lamphere out of stainless steel. This sculpture near the Lakota Museum outside Chamberlain, South Dakota, portrays a Lakota Native American woman. We drove on to Wahpeton, North Dakota, to tour the impressive Chahinkapa Zoo.

We journeyed to Minneapolis to the Mall of America, escaping with only one minor purchase, and watched the Twins defeat the Yankees, 8 to 6. In Milwaukee we lodged at the Muse Gallery Guesthouse and took in the Brewers losing to the Reds 14 to 6. Rolling on to Chicago, we stayed with my brother Stan and his wife Anita, and the four of us attended the musical performance of *Les Misérables*.

We traveled on to St. Louis, where we rode to the top of the Gateway Arch; visited the art museum, where we gazed at the original paintings of Paul Gauguin; rode the tram at Grant's Farm; and watched the Cardinals win against the Astros, 5 to 3. Then it was time to head back to Kansas for some rest.

Meanwhile, how was Peaches getting along with her second family? Bad news. She deposited diarrhea on their bedroom carpet the first night. She would not eat. She spent every minute in their upholstered chair. The second night was no better, as she left diarrhea on their carpet again. Glenda and I felt awful, volunteering to use some stain remover on their carpet when we got home. We considered the ultimate question, wondering if it was time to put her down. But we knew we weren't ready to pull the trigger.

Yet we had to ask, "Is it time?" I wondered how many more times I would have to endure cleaning up diarrhea for thirty minutes in the middle of the night. It's morphing into a chore that seems more challenging all the time. I refuse to yell in the middle of the night. Glenda needs her sleep.

While we were in a holding pattern from over a thousand miles away, praying about what to do, things got better. Reports from Rachel were that Peaches was eating again. Guess who was feeding her? Yes, Bentley. She was moving around with no results of any loose stools.

At the end of our trip, we pulled into Kevin and Rachel's driveway, aware that they needed to leave for a banquet any minute. We gave Bentley a Cardinals jersey and a dinosaur toy that blew bubbles. We talked about our trip. Then we heard barking from the basement where Peaches was kept. Kevin went to pick her up, and she was overjoyed to see us. She celebrated with her bubbly spin cycle. She had missed us, and we had missed her. She wanted me to hold her. Wish granted.

Once we got her home, she was back to the normal dog we had known. She ate and drank. No loose stools for the next month. She got excited about her walk. She has not shown any sign of illness or weakness since we have come home.

As the last update sounded too good to be true, Peaches showed more aging problems. She was closer to 102, and she frustrated Glenda and me with her inability to control her bowels. Glenda had shampooed the carpet to cover the smell and looks of the last round of her accidents. We let her out twice in the morning to poop. She could not go then. A subtle hint came when she would not eat her treat that morning. She came right back into the house and left her handiwork all over the house. I was at work by then, so Glenda inherited the joy of cleanup.

Five ragged bath towels spread out in the living room and master bedroom over the pet spray deodorizer portrayed a visible reminder of our doggy's accidents. When Peaches had the problem of bowel movements in the house before, Glenda looked for a solution. She said, "Maybe it's the soft food."

We cut back on the soft food. I took five cans of soft food back to the vet's office. They were kind about giving me a refund, but the problem persisted.

"No more table food," Glenda said. We cut back on the table food and gave her fewer treats. Again, no change. We concluded it wasn't what she was eating but a problem with aging.

Peaches started looking like a skeleton, with nothing visible but bones sticking out. Glenda was concerned about how skinny Peaches appeared. She said, "Eating nothing but hard food would get old fast. Maybe we should try soft food again."

Reluctantly, I went back to the vet's office, sure they would pro-claim me crazy for asking to buy the same cans of soft food I had just returned. They were congenial about it. We tried the soft food again. No problems plagued us for the first two feedings, but the third time Peaches gulped down the soft food, the same old disaster exploded.

Glenda had reached her limit, and I wasn't far from mine. She said, "I can't trust her. She will be sleeping in the utility room from now on." Ironically, she started out in the utility room with the washer and dryer when we first got her. That was five moves ago. The circle of life nudged her back to where she started.

"Good night, Peaches. Have sweet dreams. We love you," I said, as I tucked her into her basket. For the first time in many years, I went to bed without Peaches sleeping beside me. It seemed strange she was absent. Meanwhile, she snoozed in her basket in the utility room.

She showed grace in understanding her lot as she began to sleep in the utility room. It was impressive how easily Peaches accepted sleeping in the utility room—no barking or dirty looks to protest. That lasted one week. She must have thought that arrangement was only temporary.

Exactly one week later, I carefully placed her in her basket in the utility room. I gave her a good-night kiss and said, "Sleep good. Sweet dreams. I love you."

She gave me a look intended to kill. Her message implied, "What? You're going to keep me in this Alcatraz for another night? I've had enough of these sleeping quarters."

Her separation anxiety was again rearing its ugly head. She need-ed my touch and didn't want to be shunned from it. Minutes later, after I had turned in for the night and was starting to doze off, Peaches began to bark and moan. Not in a loud way, but just barely loud enough for us to hear.

"Peaches is barking," said Glenda.

"Let her bark," I replied.

Neither Glenda nor I made any move toward the utility room. After ten minutes of relaying her message, Peaches got quiet and went to sleep.

Ah, the ups and downs of owning a dog! Peaches earned some good behavior time in her prison cell that helped her get released. She went three weeks without one accident in the house. We rewarded her good behavior by allowing her to sleep against her owner's left calf again.

Still, other aging problems plagued her. She had another illness. While Peaches shook uncontrollably, she wouldn't leave her basket or touch her treat. Perhaps God was preparing me for something. Maybe God was preparing Peaches for something.

Other patterns from her advancing age emerged to suggest her days were numbered. On a ten-minute drive to Rachel's house, she slept the entire way. In the past, she watched the scenery the entire route. "Walk" was still the magic word that fired her up, exciting her no end. On the return trip, though, she dragged it out as if she had all day. This old dog has not learned any new tricks, especially how to arrive home in thirty minutes.

She ate well one day; the next day, she didn't. The change in her sleeping quarters forced us to recognize that the day when we have to put her down was not far off, even though Glenda and I clung to the hope Peaches would stay with us for a lot more time.

We struggled so much in dealing with the 180-degree changes that suggested her life was inching toward its end. It hit me like the Kansas tornado that swept Dorothy and her sparkling red shoes off her feet, and I cried the whole time Peaches and I walked. I needed some caulking to mend the cracks in my broken heart. What made it unbearable was that she still understood things mentally. She still heard. She still saw.

One day, I thought everything went well for Peaches, and the next day, I realized it didn't. The Bible reminds us how short life can be. David emphasizes the brevity of life in Psalm 103:14–16. He writes,

For he [God] knows how we are formed,

He remembers that we are dust.

The life of mortals is like grass,

They flourish like a flower of the field;

The wind blows over it and it is gone,

And its place remembers it no more.

James, half-brother of Jesus, adds, "You are a mist that appears for a little while and then vanishes" (James 4:14c). For a dog, divide the years by seven, and its life is even shorter.

We wanted to offer each one in our family the chance to say good-bye. Once family members had expressed their farewells, I planned to call Clinton Skaggs, DVM, and schedule an appointment. I wanted to request that Dr. Skaggs allow me to hold her as she is euthanized to prevent her from feeling all alone as she is ushered into heaven. I wanted to help allay her fears.

"Accept the grief, never the guilt." That challenge awaited as I tried to put my own words into practice. Peaches seemed to be content as she looked ahead to a home where she will find no more suffering, no more tears, no more death.

The calendar said she had turned 102 years old, but her clock was still ticking. We were more aware of how much we appreciated our remaining time with her. Just knowing that our time with her was gradually dwindling, I became more willing to show patience with her and looked for ways to show my love for her. We kept our fingers crossed about when that day that makes us shudder would come, but we still remembered to enjoy the time we had left. We gave thanks for her health and for the time we spent with her. We thanked God for the lessons she had taught us.

After all our preparation for the worst, Peaches made a new 180-degree turn. She had no problem controlling her bowels for three weeks. No accidents in the house. She barked, alerting us when she needed to go outside. She was herself again—excited about our walks, eating well, yet still sleeping more than she used to. After watching this, I changed my mind to believe that she was simply going through illness and separation anxiety when staying with Kevin, Rachel, and Bentley.

I couldn't blame it all on age. As Peaches turned 102, I thought at first that age did not seem to be a problem for her. Might I remember her lesson as Father Time makes more and more regular visits, I thought.

Our aging adventures with Peaches have left me feeling like a yo-yo going up and down with her good days and bad days. The latest bad news is that after over a month of Peaches' refraining from any accidents, the diarrhea began again, resulting in major cleanup. I took back all I said about how aging hasn't affected her.

Then Peaches was able to keep away from rectal disaster for another week and a half. She earned good time again and wasn't forced to sleep in the utility room. It felt great that she slept beside me again.

Yet other physical problems persisted. She had trouble going down steps, waiting at the top of the stairs and hesitating to go down. She tried to jump up into my Camry and crashed. She didn't yelp and tried again. She limped. She wanted her walk each day but failed to last very long, walking at a snail's pace. I had to carry her home more often. She approached the stairs very slowly, once falling down three stairs from the utility room to the garage. She showed all the signs and symptoms of arthritis and osteoporosis.

Peaches was able to see, but a cataract covered her right eye. Glenda and I watched as she walked directly into the right rear tire on Glenda's car. She didn't yelp but backed up and ran into the same tire again. She made more trips into the street than she used to. She stood still in the driveway and looked forlorn throughout a five-minute lapse. These signs of old age, as well as her brief life, served as reminders that eventually old age catches up with all of us.

Cancer is the number one cause of death in dogs over ten years of age, afflicting over half of dogs past that age. We found over half of the symptoms for cancer debilitating Peaches, including sluggishness, inflexible legs, pain, dark spots under her fur, unusual smells coming from her mouth, loss of appetite, rapidly declining weight and frequent urinating.

Soon after Peaches turned 104, after watching Peaches waddle down the driveway, after she no longer walked three houses away to the mailbox, after we watched her sleep her days away, after her incontinence became a problem, after we shampooed carpets much too often, after Peaches rejected allowing Autumn to trim her face, after we had put off the inevitable as long as we could, after it was obvious her quality of life was gone, we knew the saddest day had come. It was time.

That difficult decision was confirmed on January 9, 2020, when Peaches woke me up at four in the morning. She jumped from her sleep with a moan of pain. She was hurting. This was more than any dream. I picked her up and carried her outside to potty. She gawked around for a couple of minutes as if she didn't know what to do. Then she hobbled down to the fire hydrant dividing our lawn from the neighbor's and spent three minutes sniffing and marking. Peaches walked halfway up the driveway, where she stopped and looked at me. Her confused gaze implied, "Aren't you going to help me?"

I began to weep before getting her bedded down again. And went through half a box of tissues, my face wet with tears.

January 10, 2020, is the day that will live on in infamy in my memory. On a positive note, however, it was the day we got to end her pain and suffering, the day Saint Peter said, "Welcome to a heavenly home, a place where you will never suffer again."

I appreciated our good relationship with veterinarian Clinton Skaggs and made an appointment with him to have Peaches euthanized. During our seventy-mile drive to Pratt, Peaches never once looked out the window to check out the scenery. That had only happened once before.

I am convinced that she knew, that she was aware her last days on earth were almost over. Resting on my lap, she also realized there was nothing to worry about. She would soon be climbing the steps of the rainbow bridge. She was aware that the beauty and peace of heaven were only minutes away.

I arrived early and said to the receptionist, Rhea Shinkle, "I need to write you a check."

"No, you don't," Clinton replied from the side door.

Rhea handed me a tissue. Great timing. Smoke was starting to moisten my eyes. Even though my issue was grief, their kindness overwhelmed me.

Clinton gave me a bear hug. He calmly indicated that watching her getting euthanized would be too much for me. He wisely advised me to stay in the waiting room while he took her back to go ahead with the inevitable. I sat down to weep while Dr. Skaggs took Peaches to a back room.

I was greatly disappointed the plan to hold her had fallen apart. Alone, I was faced with the reality I had seen her for the last time. I had lost loved ones. I had officiated funerals for four grandparents and other family. But I had never felt immediate grief with this much pain. Yet I was also sure Dr. Skaggs was right. I couldn't have handled it. He returned and handed me the box containing Peaches, making my voice crack.

We then talked some about our families. I talked about where our children were now and listened to an update on the whereabouts of his grown children, Delaney and Hayden. Aware of the forecast for freezing rain and snow, he encouraged me: "Be careful on the roads and hang tough."

In my time of need, he and Rhea were so comforting. But I had to pull over on the drive home. I t was too hard to see with smoke in my eyes.

It was actually Peaches who got to eat ice cream cake,
and she received this birthday card.

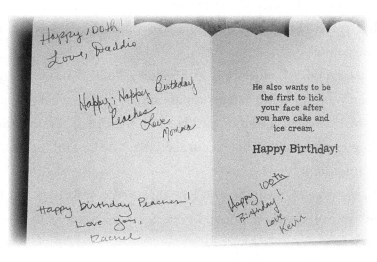

Peaches was determined to keep me from forgetting her. I had made a habit of shutting the bedroom door when going to bed, guaranteeing she would not have any accidents in the rest of the house.

Exactly two weeks to the day after her passing, I shut the same door without remembering she wasn't around anymore. Just a habit. Simultaneously, I heard a bark—not just any bark but the same sound I had heard thousands of times. Though some may be skeptical, it was clearly Peaches' bark.

She was saying, "Don't forget about me. Yes, I am better than ever. I assure you that I am in no pain."

"Thanks for letting me know, little buddy."

I could not part with the blanket Glenda had made for Peaches, so I now have pictures of lions, tigers, monkeys, giraffes, elephants, and hippos covering me at night. That blanket always goes on top. Her ashes still rest on the fireplace mantle.

Then Suzy, Mom's dachshund, passed on to her heavenly home four weeks after Peaches did. She was just a week short of her fifteenth birthday, nearing 105 in dog years. Suzy could have lived on a diet of raw carrots and broccoli stems. She loved going to the nursing home with Mom to visit the elderly.

"No more dogs," Glenda kept saying. Thank God that Glenda didn't stick to that famous quote when Peaches came to live with us.

Acknowledgments

••●••

I am immensely grateful to my family members, who have not only starred in this book but have also willingly spent time answering my questions about how it all happened. They have given me details on lots of the stories included here. So many thanks for their input go out to my wife, Glenda, and my daughters, Andrea Shultz and Rachel Steiner. My gratitude goes to my three-year-old grandson, Bentley Steiner, who made his debut in a starring role.

I am so grateful to my sister-in-law Ronda Ost and niece Abby Elkins for their patience in combing through gripping stories and sharing details about their dogs. Thank you to my brother David Ferguson and his wife, Cheryl, for taking time to tell their dog stories.

Thank you to my late father, Charles Ferguson, who always had Chihuahuas around. His innovative skills were tested when Chico delivered six tiny puppies and the last one was ushered into this world in a touch-and-go, life-or-death condition. Dad acted out of true love for the tiny puppy by gently placing the struggler in a little corn bread box, creating a homemade incubator as he heated the oven up to a safe, life-giving temperature. It worked, and the puppy survived!

Thank you to my late mother, Violet Schott, who also cared for dogs, including a Chihuahua, a German shepherd, and two dachshunds. Her wiener dog, Suzy, made all the recent family pictures. A dog greatly loved by Mom and Milt, she was born on Valentine's Day, just eleven days before Peaches. Some of Mom's care for dogs came at times when she was the only caretaker in the household, qualifying her for another star in her crown.

Both of my parents were tremendous examples of how to treat a dog. Many more family members deserve words of gratitude.

A huge shout-out has been earned by Peaches, the best dog I've ever had, in spite of my original unwillingness to accept her. Sorry I didn't welcome you at first. I am eternally grateful for my time with Peaches. I had finished writing this book before she passed. Going through the grief of missing her has been a slow process. Aware of the need for rewrites, I resisted them for two years and two months— even longer than the two years that counseling experts say it takes to come down from the shock of losing a closely loved family member.

I am grateful to the supporting cast listed in the order they appear, all of whom are my heroes: Stevie, Augie, Bullseye, Suzy, Lady Luck, Lacey, "DOG," King, Laya, Luke, Chervey, Jagger, Lady, Tramp, Angel, Scamp, Buster, Jock, Reggie, Trusty, Kramer, Paisley, Hawkeye, Lindsey, Millie the Weather Dog, Old Yeller, Ellie, Roscoe, Molly, Hosmer, Charlie, Ruby, Tate, Chico, Taco, Poco, Tina, Ranger, Gretchen, Odin, Tessa, Balto, Friday, Wishbone, Toto, Higgins, Roselle, Salty, Hachiko, Kamikaze-go, Go-Go, Canelo, Nova, Laika, Zori, Frida, Charm, Buck, Belle, Scooter, Smoky, Sadie, Bella, Lassie, Rin Tin Tin, Rin Tin Tin Jr., Rin Tin Tin III, Rin Tin Tin IV, Rin Tin Tin XII, Strongheart, Zach, Oscar, Tasha, Capitan, and Trixie.

I am blessed by many breeds who contributed in a loving way to this book. They include the Golden retriever, Labrador retriever, collie, bull terrier, dachshund, Shetland sheepdog, Chihuahua, Labrador, Weimaraner, Maltese, poodle, German shepherd, Shih Tzu, Highland white terrier, Afghan hound, Irish setter, schnauzer,

Pembroke Welsh corgi, mastiff, cocker spaniel, English setter, Cavalier King Charles spaniel, Jack Russell terrier, Cairn terrier, rat terrier, Great Pyrenees, Akita, Doberman pinscher, Canary mastiff, Belgian Malinois, Chesapeake Bay retriever, greyhound, Yorkshire terrier, springer spaniel, Pomeranian, French bulldog, and Havanese.

Designer dogs not recognized as breeds by the AKC include gold-endoodles and, of course, Maltipoos. Oscar, the mutt of the fifty-seven varieties, cannot be left out.

If your dog's breed has been omitted in this list, I apologize. One dog handbook that I perused described over three hundred different breeds, but describing every one of the breeds was never a goal of this book.

Thank you to Autumn Hanson for having the patience and for-titude to take great care of Peaches as her most excellent groomer. Thank you to Clinton Skaggs, DVM, and receptionist Rhea Shinkle for going the extra mile in caring for Peaches. My appreciation goes out to Kate Vanden Hull, DVM, for her kindness in caring for Belle.

I am overwhelmingly grateful to a former administrative assis-tant, Frances Zellers, who was always willing to drop everything and help me with my lack of technical skills. Thank you to Linda Broce, who shared the anonymous prose work titled "Rules of the House (Regarding the Dog)" found at the end of chapter 4 ("Who's Training Who?").

I am eternally grateful to Palmetto Publishing and their excel-lent staff. Thank you so much to project manager Kristin Graham, who always had the answers to my questions; line editor Betty, who shared many great ideas to improve the manuscript and taught me so much; Josie Guinn, who welcomed me aboard; the cover illustrator, who designed two gorgeous covers for me to choose from; the layout designer; and the marketing advisor. What a kind, discerning staff!

Thanks be to God, who was able to help place words on my screen when my brain was fatigued and blank.

About the Author

••●••

Dan E. Ferguson has published another book titled *Grace's Mirror: Healing for Perfectionists* that received a five-star rating on Amazon and is recommended by counselors. He is a member of the American Association of Christian Counselors and certified as a mental health life coach. He holds a doctorate of ministry in pastoral counseling from the Graduate Theological Foundation.

Over the past forty-three years, he has served as pastor of thirteen United Methodist Churches: five large, three tiny, and five in between.

His passion is riding a bicycle—he has logged enough miles to circle the equator three times over the past fifteen years, not counting a ten-month absence when COVID-19 first hit. Dan foresees no plans to complete a fourth trip. He enjoys playing golf and rooting for the Kansas City Chiefs, Kansas Jayhawk basketball, St. Louis Cardinals, Kansas City Royals, St. Louis Blues, Sporting KC, and many more.

He treasures his time with his wife, Glenda, daughter Rachel Steiner and her husband Kevin, and daughter Andrea Shultz and her husband Jeff, and he cherishes three growing grandchildren: Bentley (aged six years), Hartley (three), and Mia Grace (three). When Dan's coffee doesn't revive him, he looks for these three live wires to slap some high fives on. His energy immediately skyrockets.

Notes

Introduction

[1] Nick Trout, *Love Is the Best Medicine: What Two Dogs Taught One Veterinarian about Hope, Humility, and Everyday Miracles* (New York: Broadway Books, 2010), xii.

[2] Ibid.

[3] Gary D. Sherman and Jonathan Haidt, "Research Has Found That People Who Talk To Pets Are Smarter Than Those Who Don't," The Science of Positivity, Harvard University, August 18,2018. https://www.thescienceofpositivity.com/research-has-found-that-people-who-talk-to-pets-are-smarter-than-those-who-dont/

[4] Brian Pascus, "Dog Ownership Linked to Longer Life in Two New American Heart Association Studies," CBS News, October 5, 2019. https://www.cbsnews.com/news/dog-ownership-linked-to-longer-life-after-heart-attack-and-stroke-american-heart-association-studies-find/

[5] Dhruv Kazi, "How a Dog Can Help You Live Longer, Lower Your Blood Pressure and Make You Healthier," *Washington Post*, October 12, 2019. https://www.scmp.com/lifestyle/health-wellness/article/3032356/how-dog-can-help-you-live-longer-lower-your-blood

[6] Ibid.

1
No More Dogs
[1] Robert Fulghum, *Maybe (Maybe Not)* (New York: Villar Books, 1993), 71.

[2] Ibid., 73.

[3] Ibid., 74.

[4] Ibid.

2
King Survives
[1] Stanley Coren, *The Intelligence of Dogs: A Guide to the Thoughts, Emotions, and Inner Lives of Our Canine Companions* (New York: Bantam Books, 1994), 182

[2] Justine A. Lee, "Top 10 Poisons of 2015 Affecting Dogs and Cats," VETgirl, March 1, 2015.
https;//www.cbsnews.com/news/dog-ownership-linked-to-longer-life-after-heart-attack-and-stroke-amrican-heart-association-studies-find/
[3] Ibid.

[4] Tom Sykes, "Barking Mad: Crufts Dog Show Murder Mystery Deepens; Were Two Sheepdogs Poisoned?" Daily Beast, March 10, 2015. https://www.thedailybeast.com>canine-murder-hits-crufts-dog-show

[5] WebMD Pet Health Center, June 21, 2022. https://www.americanhumane.org/fact-sheet/pets/poisons/

[6] Lee, "Top 10 Poisons."

[7] "Substances Poisonous to Dogs," Wikipedia. https://en.wikipedia.org/wiki/Substances_poisonous_to_dogs

3

Fear the Dogcatcher

[1] Misty King, interviewed on "The BTK Killer Speaks," A&E Documentary Special, 2005. https://aetv.com/shows/btk-confessions-of-a-serial-killer

[2] Mark D. Griffiths, "The Psychology of Animal Torture: Why Would Anyone Want to Deliberately Inflict Pain on Animals?" *Psychology Today*, November 23, 2016. http://www.psychologytoday.com/us/blog/in-excess/201611/the-psychology-animal/torture

[3] Shirley Zindler, "The Secret Life of Dog Catchers: The Story of My Life As an Animal Control Officer and My Passion to Make a

Difference," Kickstarter, January 28, 2013. https://www.kickstarter.com/projects/156168057/the-secret-life-of-dog-catchers

[4] Ibid.

4

Who's Training Who?
[1] Lauren Cahn, "25 Dogs That Don't Shed (That Much)," Reader's Digest website,
January 19, 2020.
https://www.msn.com/en/us/lifestyle/
pets/25-dog-breeds-that-dont-shed-that-much/ss-BB15J4GS_

[2] Ibid.

[3] "Anonymous, Rules of the House (Regarding the Dog), based on "Ten Dog Rules" in "Funny Joke of the Day,"Smilezilla, January 22, 2018. Smilezilla.com

5

Andrea's Crowd
[1] Emily Younger, "Wichita Dog Tubes on Lake," KSNW, Channel 3, Wichita, Kansas,
August 30, 2019.
https://www.ksn.com/news/local/
video-wichita-dog-tubes-on-lake/

[2] Mark Duell and Laurie Whitwell, "Happy ending for Hawkeye: Dog who lay by his Navy SEAL master's coffin during funeral finds a new home with best friend, "*Daily Mail*, August 26, 2011. https://www.dailymail.co.uk/news/article-2030304/Happy-ending-Hawkeye-Dog lay-Navy-SEAL-masters-coffin-funeral-finds-new-home-best-friend-html

6

Lindsey Runs Away

[1] "Ross Janssen, Eyewitness News Says Goodbye to Millie 'The Weather Dog,'" KWCH TV, Channel 12, Wichita, Kansas, May 17, 2019. https://www.ktvh.com/content/news/KWCH-12-Eyewitness-News-says goodbye-to-Millie-The-Weather-Dog-510078281.html

[2] "The Queen's Royal Corgis," Wikipedia. https://www.akc.org/expert-advice/lifestyle/the-queens-royal corgis/

[3] Ross Janssen, "Remembering Millie: Ross Shares How Millie Passed Her Employee Evaluation with Flying Colors," KWCH TV, Channel 12, Wichita, Kansas, May 17, 2019.

[4] Melissa Scheffler, "Remembering Millie: Melissa Scheffler Relives Sharing the Green Screen with Millie," KWCH TV, Channel 12, Wichita, Kansas, May 17, 2019. https://www.facebook.com/Remembering-Millie-109306750493786/

5 Ross Janssen, "Eyewitness News Says Goodbye to Millie 'The Weather Dog,'" KWCH TV, Wichita, Kansas, May 17, 2019.

6 Janae Jones, "How dogs increase productivity and happiness un the workplace," Button Tap, August 26,2018. *Good Morning America* scrolled the crawler on June 5, 2020.
https://blog.usebutton.com/
how-dogs-increase-productivity-and-happiness-in-the-workplace

7 Michael Schwanke, "Eyewitness News Says Goodbye to 'Millie the Weather Dog,'" KWCH TV, Channel 12, Wichita, Kansas, May 17, 2019.

8 Ibid.

9 Ross Janssen, "Eyewitness News Says Goodbye to Millie 'The Weather Dog,'" KWCH TV, Channel 12, Wichita, Kansas, May 17, 2019.

7

Sneaking into the Motel
1 Bruce Fogle, *Dog Breed Handbook* (New York: Dorling Kindersley Publishing, 1997), 6.

2 Ibid., 9.

9

Barking Chihuahuas

[1] Amanda Harding, "The Best Dog Breeds for People Who Work All Day," American Kennel Club Culture Cheat Sheet, August 3, 2018,
https://www.cheatsheet.com/culture/the-best-dog-breeds-for-people-who-work-all-day.html/

[2] Ibid.

[3] "The 30 Most Dangerous Dogs You Don't Want to Mess With," City of Swan, Washington.
https://www.swan.wa.gov.au/Your-Services/Animals/Dogs/Dangerous-dogs-restricted-breeds

[4] Ibid.

10

A Warm-Hearted Sidekick

[1] Sarah Heise, "Hero dog saves goats, deer from raging Tubbs Fire in Santa Rosa," KCRA3-TV, Sacramento, California, October 16, 2017.
https://www.kcra.com/article/hero-dog-saves-goats-deer-from-raging-tubbs-fire-in-santa-rosa/1309671

[2] Lauren McDevitt, as quoted by Carolyn Steber in "The 9 Best Dog Breeds for Emotional Support Animals,"

Bustle, May 31, 2019. https://www.bing.com/images/
search?q=carolynsteber+"the+best+breeds+for+emotional+
support+animals"&go=Search&qs=ds&form=QBIR&-
first=1&tsc=imageHoverTitle

[3] Aleita Downer, "Characteristics of Therapy Dogs," Cape-Able
Canines, San Diego, as quoted by Melissa Joseph in *Moments with
Baxter* (San Diego, California: Sage Press, 2009), 209.

[4] Ibid.

[5] Margaret Renkl, "What It Means to Be Loved by a Dog," *New
York Times*, June 18, 2018.
https://margaretrenkl.com/essay/what-it-means-to-be-loved-by-a-
dogby-margaret-renklthe-new-york-times-18-june-2018/

[6] Ibid.

[7] Ibid.

[8] Ibid.

[9] Elise Lufkin and Diana Walker, *Second Chances: More Tales of Found
Dogs* (Guilford, Connecticut: Lyons Press, 2003), 3.

[10] Ibid.

11
Outfoxing Jack Russell
[1] Coren, *Intelligence of Dogs*, 182

[2] Ibid.

[3] Michael Hingson with Susy Flory, *Thunder Dog: The True Story of a Blind Man, His Guide Dog, and the Triumph of Trust at Ground Zero* (Nashville, Tennessee: Thomas Nelson Publishers, 2011), title

[4] Ibid., 81, as quoted in Julio E. Correa, "The Dog's Sense of Smell," Alabama Cooperative Extension System website, Alabama A&M and Auburn Universities, July, 2005. https://ssl.acesag.auburn.edu/pubs/docs/U/UNP-0066.-archive.pdf

[5] Hingson and Flory, *Thunder Dog*, 16.

[6] Ibid., 172.

[7] Ibid., 139.

12
Kidney Stone Disaster
[1] Peter Dobias, "Bladder and Kidney Stones and Urine Crystals in Dogs—Natural Approach," March 7, 2014. https://peterdobias.com/blogs/blog/11014185-bladder-and-kidney-stones-and-urine-crystals-in-dogs-natural-approach

[2] Ibid.

[3] Peta Owens-Liston, "Kidney Stones: Very Scary True Stories. And Entombed Mysteries," *Science Communications*, ARUP Laboratories, Salt Lake City, Utah, October 1, 2015. https://www.aruplab.com/news/10-o1-15

[4] Ibid.

[5] Ibid.

15

Always Buddies

[1] Martha Sherill, *Dog Man: An Uncommon Life on a Faraway Mountain* (New York: Penguin Press, 2008), 2.

[2] Ibid., 3.

[3] Ibid., 5.

[4] "Hachi: A Dog Tale," Wikipedia. https://en.wikipedia.org/wiki/Hachi_A_Dog%27s_Tale

16

Food Hound

[1] Dhobi Ka Kutta, "DOG or GOD: Canelo 12 Years on the Hospital Door Waiting for his Friend to Come Out!!!," Media Laundry, May 8, 2012. https://www.bing.com/

search?q=Dhobi%2Ka%20Kutta%20"Dog%20or%20
God%3ACanelo&qs=ds&form=QBRE

17
Her Sense of Smell

[1] James Walker, "How to Teach Your Dog to Find Things in 7 Easy Steps," German Shepherd Shop, May 13, 2020. https://www.germanshepherdshop.com/blogs/list/how-to-teach-your-dog-to-find-things-in-7-easy-steps

[2] Ibid.

[3] Ibid.

[4] Dan Garrett, "PARTNERS IN CRIME: abused dog finds FURever home with Geary County Lieutenant," KSNTV, March 26, 2019. https://www.ksnt.com/news/partners-in-crime-abused-dog-finds-furever-home-with-geary-county-lieutenant/

[5] Ibid.

[6] Samantha Bubar, "Common Issues with Rescue Dogs," Wide Open Pets, February 21, 2020. https://aptrinhx.com/news/common-issues-with-rescue-dogs-LPDl01B/

[7] Tori Ann Oursler, "Adopting Out Aggressive Dogs," VetzInsight, February 17, 2016.
https://www.northeastanimalshelter.org/wp-content/uploads/2018/04/Adopting-Out-Aggressive-Dogs.pdf

[8] Ibid.

[9] Janet Scarlett, as quoted by Susan Kahler in "Unmasking the Shelter Dog," JAVMA News, American Veterinary Medical Association website, March 18, 2015, https://www.avma.org/javma-news/2015-04-01/unmasking-shelter-dog.

[10] Maia Belay, "OSU Study Reveals Which Dog Breeds Most Likely to Bite, How Severe Injuries Could Be," Fox 8 Cleveland, May 30, 2019.
https://fox8.com/news/osu-study-ranks-which-dog-breeds-most-likely-to-bite-and-how-severe-injuries-could-be/

[11] Julia Thompson, "Intro to Search and Rescue Dogs," THATMUTT.com. https://www.bing.comSearch?9=Julia+Thompson+"Intro+to+Search+and+Rescue+Dogs"+-form=WNSGPH=qs=SW+child=87fce81e8c41979bcc7cf-723b3e3f98+pq=Julia+Thompson+"Intro+to+Search

[12] Amanda Littlejohn, "Dogs That Save Lives: Facts About Search-and-Rescue Dogs," PetHelpful, March 6, 2019. https://www.bing.comSearch?q=Amanda+Little-

john%2C+"Dogs+That+Save+Lives%3A=Facts+about+-
Search+Rescue+Dogs+form=WNSGPH+qs

[13] Danielle Garrand, "Frida the Rescue Dog—Who Became a
Symbol of Hope after Deadly Mexico Earthquake—Retires," CBS
News, June 25, 2019. https://www.cbsnews.com/news-frida-dog-
mexico-frida-the-hero-rescue-dog-eho-became-a-symbol-of-hope-
after-deadly-mexico-earthquake-retires/

[14] Agence France-Presse (AFP), as quoted by Garrand in "Frida the
Rescue Dog."

[15] Remezcla, as quoted by Garrand in "Frida the Rescue Dog.".

21
Yorkies: Belle and Scooter

[1] Eric Alvarez, "Loyal dogs rescue owner after stroke: Ring
camera captures all," First Coast News at 6:00, Jacksonville,
Florida, February 4, 2019. https://www.nbcnews.com/video/
stroke-victim-saved-by-her-dogs-in-florida-home-1437610051841

[2] Ibid.

[3] Ibid.

[4] Ibid.

32
People Left Behind

[1] Joe Yonan, "The Death of a Pet Can Hurt As Much As the Loss of a Relative," *New York Post*, March 26, 2012. https://www.animalhealthfoundation.org/blog/2016/09/the-death-of-a-pet-can-hurt-as-much-as-the-loss-of-a-relative/

[2] Ibid.

[3] Ibid.

[4] Ibid.

[5] Adam Clark, "7 Self-Care Essentials While Grieving the Loss of a Dog," *Psychology Today*, February 13, 2017. https://www.psychologytoday.com/us/blog/animal-atachment/201702/7-self-care-essentials-while-grieving-the-death-pet

[6] Mark Breitenberg, "Losing a Pet Is More Painful Than Most People Think," *Science*, May 1, 2019. https://thelifehacker.org/2019/06/17/losing-a-pet-is-more-painful-than-most-people-think/

[7] Ibid.

[8] Bhvishya Patel, "Vet Pens Heartbreaking Letter about What It Is Like to Put Down a Pet," *Daily Mail* website, October 5, 2019.

https://www.dailymail.co.uk/femail/article-7538137/Vet-pens-
heartbreaking-letter-like-euthanize-animal.html

[9] Ibid.

[10] Dean Koontz, *A Big Little Life: A Memoir of a Joyful Dog Named Trixie* (New York: Hyperion Books, 2009), 259–265.

[11] Ibid., 264–265.

[12] Ibid., 265.

[13] Ibid.

[14] Ibid.

33

Kind Dogs in Heaven

[1] Eben Alexander, *Proof of Heaven: A Neurosurgeon's Journey into the Afterlife* (New York: Simon and Schuster Paperbacks, 2012), 71.

[2] Jennifer Skiff, *The Divinity of Dogs: True Stories of Miracles Inspired by Man's Best Friend* (New York: Atria Books, 2012), 5.

[3] James Herriot, *All Creatures Great and Small* (New York: St. Martin's Press, 1972), 270–271.

[4] Ibid.

CPSIA information can be obtained
at www.ICGtesting.com
Printed in the USA
LVHW080829281122
733860LV00008B/556

9 798885 906593